Before You
Wreck Yourself

Also by the Author
Matt Livingston, You Liar!

Before You Wreck Yourself

One Man's Three-Year Recovery from Divorce

Matt Omega

E. L. Marker
Salt Lake City

E. L. Marker, an imprint of WiDo Publishing
Salt Lake City, Utah
www.widopublishing.com

This book is a work of creative nonfiction. It is a product of the author's memory, which is flawed. Several names and personal details have been changed; others have not.

Cover mandala designed by Kelly Livingston in collaboration with the author
Book design by Marny K. Parkin
Mandala PNG by mongkol kornkamol from Vecteezy.com

ISBN: 978-1-947966-70-3

Dedication

RECOVERING FROM DIVORCE IS HARD. I DEDICATE this book to all the guardian angels who helped me along the way:

My Sister Kelly Livingston, who always rolled with me on the good days and the bad, finding portals to adventure at each city intersection, and in one of her quippy reality checks gave me the name for this book.

My assiduous and loving Mom, Lisa Livingston.

My stalwart yet sensitive Dad, John Livingston.

My immortal hero Brother, Kyle Livingston.

Our two other radiant Sisters, Lindsay Livingston and Morgan Lee.

My Best Friend, Dan.

My favorite lovebirds, Francesco and Jess.

My yoga teachers: Marsha, Kathy, Suzanne, Diana, Rob, Jo-Lynn, Alan, and Cleve.

My memoir maven, Hollis Gillespie.

My energy healer and spirit guide, Beka.

My supportive publisher, Karen Gowen.

My candid and insightful editors, Tamara and William.

And to my Mintakan mermaid, the one who was with me in my heart all along, patiently waiting for the events in this book to unfold, my twin flame, Alissa Melody Omega.

Contents

Chapter 1

How to Get Divorced

I WOKE UP ON SATURDAY, SEPTEMBER 24, 2016, expecting to go to bed feeling hated.

I had just left my wife and told the world around us that we were getting divorced.

Being hated was what I thought I deserved. I hated myself for failing at marriage and figured I would get that same disdain from others.

Instead, I felt loved. I felt a love I hadn't surrendered to in my entire adult life. Friends and family were seeing me at what I thought was my worst: getting divorced and possibly an adulterer. They were supporting and celebrating my decision.

I expected to feel anxiety and sadness, rejection and loss. And while I judged myself, from the moment I told Karen we were getting a divorce, I felt a huge burden lifted. I felt hopeful and free. I told my family, and they cheered me on. I told my friends, and they said, "Good for you."

It felt wrong to feel so good about something bad. I realized how easy it was for me to default to feeling bad. I hadn't felt truly good in a long time. I didn't remember what it felt like. In my new vulnerable situation, I started to feel the beginning of something good.

I still had a long way to go.

Most of the friends I called had already been contacted by Karen. She went to Utah a few days before I did and spent her week in Utah rallying her troops. Not even one of them asked me if I was having an affair. I did put some thought into that ahead of time. I made sure never to meet Nikki outside of the Imaca office until after Karen and I had legally separated. The dregs of our marriage manifesting in what sadly amounted to an emotional affair, more as an excuse to put an end to the dying animal that was our nuptials, than the meaningful embrace of strangers this romance probably deserved.

I called my bishop from church. Karen had already called and told him to kick me out. I was back home in Atlanta from my impulsive Utah trip in time for church the next day. I met with our bishop right after our regular meetings. He asked me about the boys, and I didn't have an answer. I knew going into this that the hardest part would be putting my boys through the pain of divorce.

I would doubt my decision to get divorced repeatedly because of the boys. I was on my own little island out in Georgia with few friends and no family. When we moved to the Atlanta area the year before, my dad introduced me to an old pilot friend from FIT who helped me try to get some job interviews at Delta Air Lines. I remembered he was divorced. Desperate to validate my difficult decision and to get out of my own painful thoughts, I texted him, not certain what to expect in return. He texted back, "Kids need parents." Not the validation I hoped for, but it was the feedback I needed. I cried until my body started shaking, terrified of the consequences my actions would have on my kids. As the fear dissipated after what felt like hours, and my lips tasted salty like I had just emerged from an ocean swim, somehow even more tears came. I cried more violently than before, judging myself for deciding to marry someone only to eventually walk away. I felt so betrayed by myself. I cried all night until the light of dawn started creeping through the shutters, and finally fell asleep on the sofa feeling like a broken person. I cried because after all this, rather than be accountable for my decision to get a divorce, I found someone to peg it on instead. My self-image was crumbling. I knew the pilot was right. But I knew I would not be the dad I needed to be for my boys if I stayed married to their mom.

Still searching for some catharsis when I awoke late in the morning, I called a former co-worker who used to talk about his divorce every single day. "Hey, Scott." I choked back tears. "I'm getting a divorce, man, and just wanted to ask in retrospect if there's anything you'd do differently or any advice you have?"

"Sorry to hear that, Matt," Scott said. "You're a great guy and extremely talented, and you have a great career ahead of you. She's gonna try to take everything. Cancel your credit cards, close your bank account, anything in your name. Call and cancel it." Even though this was a simple task, I felt too numb to do anything. I was used to Karen spending all our money, so I wrote "cancel cards" on a note of things to do *later*. I had important questions about *now*.

"How do you even get divorced?" I asked, more desperate than curious.

"Well, first you get a lawyer," he stated flatly. "Plan on around twenty grand, maybe more, depending how difficult she gets. You'll try to come to an agreement without going to court, but she won't take it. You should file first. That will give you the upper hand. It just sucks. It absolutely totally really sucks. Good luck!"

I wrote "get lawyer" and "file first" above "cancel cards" in the *now* section of my note. Divorce was sounding complicated. And expensive! When our company first hired Scott in January 2016, he had to switch to our health insurance. The provider misfiled something he needed to correct, because he was responsible for covering his daughter's health insurance per his divorce agreement. She had a difficult preexisting condition that required an expensive medication, and because of the filing discrepancy he couldn't get her medication. No matter how hard he tried he couldn't get them to fix it. Every day for about three weeks, I heard about his insurance problem. Every conversation turned into a divorce problem. His daughter's illness, the expensive medication, and the insurance issues all stemmed from his divorce.

The problem got worse when in February we attended a conference together and he ate too many hot wings. He had indigestion that weekend, but it worsened and turned into a stomach ulcer. Insurance wouldn't pay for his ulcer bills, and I overheard once again as he spent useless hours on the phone with countless faceless operators every day. His entire insurance file needed to be redone. Eventually he stopped making fix-it calls and just re-did everything from the beginning. Insurance finally paid for his daughter's important medication.

After hanging up with Scott, I promised myself that my divorce would not become a stomach ulcer, bleeding into its own wound on and on, as the days unfolded. No. I told myself that my divorce would be done quickly and cleanly. My divorce would set me free. I was such a fool.

Church the next day was rough. When you get married in the Church of Jesus Christ of Latter-day Saints, the highest covenant you can make is eternal marriage. I believed I was doing what I had to do, and that I hadn't broken any of my marriage covenants with God, but I still felt like a failure. The biggest decision I ever made, I screwed up. You promise to never have sex outside of marriage. I never had. I made that abundantly clear to Nikki, and she respected my decision. I needed her to take the blame, and I needed her to talk me off the cliffs of guilt I kept tiptoeing around, but I didn't need her for sex. People started asking me if I thought Karen was sleeping around. I didn't think so, but I also didn't care. Whether she was or wasn't, our failed marriage was on me. I didn't feel bad telling Karen I was in love with another woman. But I did feel bad that I failed her. I felt bad that my two little boys were far away in Utah with a mother who didn't love them and didn't want me to love them either. I knew Karen would use my sons to hurt me in any way that she could, as she had so often used them to hurt my parents and other relatives for years. I remembered the morning my mom came over at 6 a.m. to see Rex before Karen woke up. I remembered the Christmas she screamed at my sister and Dad while I was at the gym with my brother Kyle, and the empty hotel we drove off to once I rushed home. I forced these thoughts from my mind, forced out the many things I could not control. I was dealing with an unpredictable, scorned woman. Nothing to control there. Let it go. Focus on controlling what I *could* control. And part of that meant staying in good standing with the church.

As I waited outside the bishop's office, a member of the local leadership walked up to me and shook my hand. My eyes cast downward in shame, I noticed he was wearing the same Cole Haan shoes as me. "I heard what you're going through, and I'm really sorry," he said. "It's going to be really hard." And then he walked off. He confirmed what I had just told myself. Time to see what the bishop, my specific local leader, said about it.

"That was a pretty heated night on Monday," said Bishop, referencing our discussion in his office the night before Karen took the boys to Utah. "As you know, Karen has already called me, but there won't be any disciplinary action here. How are you doing?"

I breathed a deep and long internal sigh of relief. I could have been ordered to receive counseling from church leaders or even been excommunicated from my church. I told my bishop the truth: I was not doing well. I needed a divorce, and the only way I could figure out how to do it was by making Karen think I was in love with someone else. She and her dad were very tricky, I told him. They were manipulative. I was afraid of their influence over me and their manipulation tactics. I had to keep myself at a distance and keep them off-balance. "I know that's all pretty messed up. So, I'll flip the question back to you. How am I doing, Bishop?"

"I think you're in a lot of pain," he said. I nodded and started to cry. I had nothing else to say. I had never felt my shoulders bob so much, so out of control, but I couldn't get them to stop galloping away up by my ears. Probably why I never cried. Crying is embarrassing. I looked up at him after a few moments.

"Do what you have to do," he summarized. "See the church psychologist again and don't break your covenants. You'll be fine."

Really? I couldn't believe what I was hearing. I thought my plan was so stupid and that nobody else would get it. I thought I would be disciplined for trying to make an emotional affair look like it was more than that, but here I was getting validation that it was okay. I made and kept a firm boundary with Nikki that our relationship would never be sexual. It seemed more and more like that was exactly the right safety measure I needed to keep everything manageable. It was never about sex for me. It hadn't been an emphasis in my marriage, and it wasn't an emphasis of my need for a divorce. I just needed out.

Within a couple days, I met with the church psychologist and told him the entire story. "So, what do you think?" I asked him. "Am I going crazy, or do I need to stop doing this with Nikki, or what?"

"Just let things run their course," he said. "I think you're doing quite well with all of this." Then he told me to write a letter to Brian Adams, Karen's dad. He said that was a common recommendation for a psychologist to give to someone who has been hurt by someone else. There are a few rules for the letter. First, nobody ever reads it. You write it and then throw it away. Next, it has no length limit or time limit. And third, it has to be completely honest. I had no idea how much I hated my father-in-law until I wrote that letter.

I realized that from my perspective, he tried to rip my whole family apart. He made me feel insecure about my relationship with my mom, and openly mocked my dad. He told me how disappointed he was in his only son, but how proud he was of me. He called me a stallion in front of the family to dissuade Karen from pursuing her PhD, telling her instead to support my ambitions. I believed he had turned me into the son he wished he had. I wrote for several pages and let it all flow out, then ripped up the letter and threw it away.

Then I thought about the boys again. I wanted them to know I loved them. I tried to Facetime them, but Karen had one of her sisters block me. I wanted to write them letters too, to somehow get it through to them that I loved them. There was no way to do it. I wanted to write the boys time-capsule letters for when they turned ten or twelve, just to tell them what I was doing and why, but I didn't do it. I needed it, but they didn't. Their mom would tell them hateful things about me, and I wouldn't do it back to her. The boys would have to look at my actions and the time I spent with them and the experiences we had as their testament of what kind of dad I was. It was better for me to be criticized by Karen and Brian behind my back, letting them do and say what they would, rather than spending another day pretending along with them.

The boys needed their dad back. The only way I could be in their lives was to sue for custody, as that became apparent when Karen and her sister blocked me whenever I tried to reach out to my kids.

That same night, Karen recounted her version of our marital situation on social media. She wrote a long post about how I was having an affair and left the church and that it was going to get ugly. I said nothing but emailed the post to my lawyer. My sister Morgan responded swiftly and directly to Karen's post on Facebook, informing Karen of some of the things she had done that hurt so many people. The next day Karen deleted the post.

Even though I didn't allow myself to care too much about the slander, my lawyer wanted me to care, to turn it into a tabloid cover story. Tom was an expert in divorce cases where the husbands and wives did devious things to each other. As he paraphrased past cases and asked me questions, some of the things Tom recounted made me blush. Sleeping with each other's relatives, making sex tapes and sending them to each other's families, he kept digging for salacious stuff in our marriage that wasn't there. I had found him on Google, he picked up on the second ring and talked to me when I needed someone to talk to. He was an expensive confidante but was always happy to talk and always happy to have his office gal Elaine bill me for it.

"Tom, all this stuff you are describing, it's just not us, man," I said. "This is a simple resentful-husband-finally-boiled-over type of divorce. That's all. And she is super pissed. Look at this." I emailed him a screenshot of the Facebook post, so he could open it on his large computer screen.

"What right does she have to drag your name through the mud?" Tom railed. "You know she's probably been sleeping around, right? They all do. Tattoos and CrossFit parties, yeah, she's sleeping around." Tom was maybe five-eight with his tall shoes on and burly like a retired Italian boxer. He had a well-manicured mustache and knew how to talk with his eyes. He would tell me something scathing he thought about Karen and then burn it into me with his eyes to make it true. "We are gonna get you divorced," Tom said near the end of each of our numerous meetings. "You need to get divorced."

Tom played into my naivete that it was some privilege to get divorced. The part of me that waited my whole life to be married for eternity, the part of me that stayed married for so long because I hadn't considered divorce an option, was still stuck in my marriage. The dogma I believed combined with my personality flaws to people-please and enable others made it hard for me to believe I deserved to be free from my marriage.

There were many times I doubted the divorce would work. In our first meeting, Tom laid out the game plan. First, we needed to file for divorce. He got that done the first day. Someone contacted Karen and served her the divorce papers. She texted me that she got them. She was surprised and upset. She was still keeping the kids away from me.

Once she was served, Tom said we should try to settle outside of the courts. I gave Tom my bank statements and pay stubs, and he made a generous offer to Karen. He got this done right away, too. It was hard, but I signed it. I would have one weeknight and every-other-weekend, as per Georgia standard divorce law.

"But Tom, she's clinically insane!" I objected before we agreed to send the offer. "She's on three medications and hates the kids!"

"Has she ever gone to jail, have you ever filed a police report?" asked Tom.

"No," I replied, thinking back to times I could have, like when she stood over me wielding a butcher knife.

"Doesn't matter," said Tom. "She'll get primary custody. If it goes to court, we can try before the judge. What she did, taking the kids out of preschool and throwing them off their routine and keeping them from you, won't sit well with the judge. But if we are going to try to settle, she's gonna want all the money she can get, and that comes along with primary custody."

We made the offer: $2600 a month in child support, an extra $1000 a month for alimony until she finished her PhD, I pay for daycare and her car and insurance. I would have very little left, but I would be free. I knew she would let me have the kids any time I wanted them. We sent the offer to Karen's lawyer.

It didn't take them half a day to ask for more. I would barely have enough to cover my bills if they took what we offered. Karen's lawyer, Anne, wanted to see my bank statements and paystubs for herself. If Tom was short, Anne was shorter. I had very little experience with lawyers, but generally thought of them as tall, commanding people. Karen and I had picked a pair that did not fit that mold. I didn't have any of the assets she kept asking about. Karen knew that. Anything I had invested in ended with marriage to Karen. Up until recently we had been poor. I was constantly juggling balance transfers on credit cards and trying to keep our bank account in the black.

It seemed that court was inevitable. And court would be tricky.

"I know Karen's lawyer pretty well," Tom jeered. "She's really short (I laughed lightly at the irony of his criticism) and just like your wife, a scorned woman who hates the Mormon Church. They'll want to cause you pain and drag this out and make you suffer."

I wasn't worried about that. Nothing she could do could rival the suffering she had put me through for the last six years.

"So how do we do it?" I asked. "How much will it cost, and how long will it take?"

"First we have to agree on a mediation date," said Tom. "We can't schedule the judge until we have gone to mediation. We know mediation won't work, right, so there's a loophole where as soon as we schedule mediation, we can schedule the judge. We mediate, go to court, he will give you a temporary order, and then a few months down the road, he will finalize it." A lump formed in my throat, and I couldn't talk or swallow. This was going to take a lot longer than I thought.

Tom continued. "You're probably looking at about twenty grand and six months." I had been warned about the cost. But six months! How was I going to do this for six months? Work was good, and I could get the money, but six months! Tom distracted me with some action items. "I'm going to get with Anne and schedule the mediation and the judge, don't worry," he said. "Here's what you need to do. First, get affidavits. A lot of them. Get as many people as you can who know both you and Karen to give you written statements that she's an unfit parent. And then you need to go get the kids. Get them back here in their regular school and on their regular routine. She won't let you see them, fuck her. Show up and take them. She has no right to keep them from you, you're their dad. They live here. Go get them back and let me know when you do."

Having these assignments took my mind off the difficult process that lay ahead. What if Anne and Karen wouldn't cooperate? If they wouldn't agree to mediate or see the judge, this could go on for years. Six months sounded long, but the more I thought about it, the more that seemed like the best-case scenario.

That's why I did what I did, I reminded myself. She didn't own me anymore. It was time to go and get some affidavits. And then, if Karen still didn't bring them back, it would be time to go get the boys.

Many of our Georgia friends had seen Karen's Facebook post. Most of them weren't fond of her and were happy to write a letter that she was unstable. Some decided to stay neutral and refused, and that was fine with me. A lot of them had divorce lawyer recommendations for me, but I didn't want to talk about it. I may not have found the best lawyer, or the cheapest lawyer, but Tom had taken my call and listened to me and told me he could get me divorced.

After making a bunch of affidavit requests, I drove home to see Karen's car parked in the driveway. We hadn't spoken in over a week, so I figured she had a friend drive it home from the airport for her.

As I approached the door, I had an eerie feeling that it was her inside the house. How could she be here while she was with the boys in Utah? Did she leave them at her parents' house while she came back to go to classes like normal? I had been angry before, but now I was livid. She took the boys away, left them with her parents, and went about her ways. Who knew what nonsense her father was filling their heads with?

I stormed into the kitchen to see Karen packing some kitchen things away in boxes. One item, the KitchenAid, cost us three hundred dollars, and she used it to make us cookies one time in our entire marriage. She demanded we buy it because she felt pressured by her mom and grandma to be a good Mormon Mom with a KitchenAid. The resentment bubbled up inside me, yet another reminder of all the things I had done to make her happy.

"What are you doing here?" I asked.

She gave me a wicked grin I had never seen before.

My eyes were wide open this time and I saw it clearly. The nights we played Rook with her parents, Karen used to jokingly say her soul was black. Black is one of the four colors in Rook. The cards are colored rather than suited, and every time someone would say "black," Karen would quickly follow with, "like my soul." She thought it was funny to say, "Black like my soul." Now I finally saw her black and twisted soul in a grin that said, "I will make you suffer for divorcing me."

My heartbeat accelerated and the hair on my neck stood up. My shoulders tightened and my hands clenched. I felt like I truly saw who she was for the first time. I could not believe I had married her and stayed with her for seven years.

She saw the look in my eyes and stopped smiling but said nothing.

I turned around and left. My resolve strengthened to follow Tom's instructions to go to Utah and bring the boys back home.

Before I left for Utah that weekend, Karen emailed me a bunch of questions like everything was normal. We agreed not to text each other anymore and move to email only. No phone calls either, only email. Texting made it too easy to respond in the heat of the moment with unnecessary back-and-forth outbursts. Emails, on the other hand, were not only easier to keep record of for legal proceedings if necessary, but since they are less "instant" they gave us a moment to cool down before responding.

She asked for more money. She'd already taken ten grand in cash and ten grand in gold, half of which was mine. I sent a few thousand dollars but told her we would have to split what she had already taken.

I flew to Salt Lake City and met Nikki for a day before going to see the boys. I needed her to hang in there with me for a little longer. She was always so happy to see me, but I could tell that beneath the nice manners she was nervous like me. We went to the mall by her house and got a prepaid burner phone we could use to communicate so there were no phone records. She was great company. She took my mind off the fact that I was ruining the marriage I spent my entire life preparing for. She distracted me from thinking I was a failure.

My brother Kyle came to meet me and drove me an hour south to hand me off to Mom and Dad. Mom volunteered to go with me the next day to pick up the boys and help us get back to Georgia. Kyle met Nikki and me briefly at Trader Joe's, and after quick introductions Kyle and I got in his car. I asked him what he thought of her.

"She's like what I would expect to see at Trader Joe's," he said. "A vegan hippie with tattoos. Not your type, bro."

I tilted my head back and belly laughed for the first time in weeks. Maybe months. I didn't know I had a "type." I married the first girl I dated after my mission at twenty-one and hadn't thought much about it in the seven years since then since.

I didn't tell Kyle anything else about her. Only my church bishop and church therapist got the full details. And they claimed they thought I was fine.

I read Kyle some of Karen's emails and vented a little bit.

"Dude, all she wants is money!" I said. "All I ever was to her was spending money, and I didn't even make that much! Hope she got what she wanted. The night before she left with the boys, I slept on the back porch swing, and kept wondering what she would do. She told me she was going to cut her wrists. I woke up early and went to the gym until her location showed she had left the house. I knew I would see the boys again soon, as much as it sucks to be away from them right now. I didn't even think about our safe for three or four days, and sure enough when I checked it, she had emptied it out. She has to give me back half of what she took."

Kyle raised his eyebrows at me while chewing down a dried mango from Trader Joe's. "Good luck getting that back!"

He was right. I was lying to myself, and I knew it. I wouldn't get any of it back. And I didn't care that much. I could laugh again. That was what mattered. She could take my money but not my happiness. Not anymore.

We met Mom and Dad at a little restaurant for lunch. They had gotten a call from my lawyer Tom earlier that morning.

"Your son is a decent man, Mrs. Livingston," Tom had told my mom. "He deserves this to work out for him and to be married to a decent woman."

We were all on the Tom-bandwagon. "Go get the kids back," Tom said, "because the judge would like that. Bring them back to their home and school. The judge will like that."

Stress levels were high as we drove down to Kanab and prepared to pick up the boys the next day. Mom wondered if we should have a guardian ad litem come with us. They are a neutral person who witnesses both families' behaviors in order to give an impartial testimony in court to help resolve custody issues. If not a guardian ad litem, maybe the police? I finally saw how terrified my parents were of Karen's dad. The father-in-law I had chosen over my own dad had divided me from them for nearly a decade. I remembered the talk my dad bravely gave me the week of my wedding to try to rescue me from what I now saw, six and a half years later, as my complete ruin.

As soon as we got home, I asked Dad if I could tell him something.

"Dad, you were right, and I am so sorry." I barely got the words out before collapsing into him in a big hug, the first we had had in far too long, sobbing onto his shoulder. "I'm sorry. I'm sorry. I'm so, so sorry."

My bicycle-pedal shoulders wouldn't stop bobbing up and down when I cried. I felt embarrassed but kept crying and shoulder-checking my dad. I kept crying around people who had never seen me cry before, and I wished I could keep the sobbing a little more under control. But I couldn't control it.

He and my mom told me about the intensive therapy they had been through while I was married. They went separately, they went together, they saw lawyers, they talked to judges. Everyone said their best move was to wait it out and do nothing but be loving and supportive. And that's what they did. They remembered more grievous experiences than I did.

My parents met over Christmas break in 1985 at BYU. Boys weren't allowed in girls dormitories, but my dad wasn't there as a student, he was there to pick up his sister, who lived on the floor where my mom was a resident assistant. Mom heard a commotion of a boy on the floor. She turned a corner to see Dad

77777777777777

standing outside his sister's room. She sternly approached him and said, "You can't be in here!"

Dad says that from the first moment he saw her, he knew she was an angel.

She turned and walked away. But she never left his mind. He drove his sister back to the ranch in Alberta and got to work. He asked his sister about what she knew about her angelic RA. He found out her full name, then her address, then her phone number. She was a thousand miles away and he only had two weeks until Christmas break would end. He was attending flight school on the other side of the continent at FIT in Melbourne, Florida. He initially drove from Melbourne to Provo, Utah, to pick up his sister, and then took them both home to the ranch in Alberta, Canada. Once he knew how to find Mom, he drove from Cardston back through Provo and all the way down Interstate 15 to La Verkin, Utah, where my mom was living with her parents. It was four thousand miles of driving in just one week.

"Come on in, smoke 'em if you've got 'em," Poppa Dale told Dad when he knocked on the door.

After a few dates with Mom, he headed back to Alberta for the rest of the break and then finally back to Florida. They kept in touch through letters and took a spring break trip to the Bahamas. Then in July they scheduled an appointment at the temple to get married. Six months and two weeks.

My maternal grandfather would live until 1999, when he would pass within twelve months of my only two uncles during the roughest emotional year of my childhood, at age eleven. I didn't know any of those three men very well. I primarily saw them during holidays. However, they were unique characters who shaped my view of what made you a man. Uncle Clayton rode horses and drove farm trucks using a knob on his steering wheel so he could turn quickly and kick up gravel at anyone who wanted to cause trouble. Uncle Kirk rode a motorcycle and had a purple Ford Probe sports car. Poppa Dale drove race cars and played basketball when he was young.

The common denominator for Mom and Dad was The Church of Jesus Christ of Latter-day Saints. My mom's Swedish ancestors on her mom's side came to Utah for the promise of religious freedom. Sadly, the more Mom learned about her past, the more she saw a pattern of powerful Church leaders using their influence to manipulate women into marrying them, and then using the name of God to force them to stay married even through cycles of abuse and neglect. This was the story of her mother, grandmother, and great-grandmother. She saw something different in Dad.

We lived in Canada for my siblings' births, and moved to Kanab, Utah, the same year of these deaths. I was supposed to start a new school and would be turning twelve, when Mormon boys started Boy Scouts and youth night at church. Instead, I wanted to cry. Why was everyone dead? Dad wanted me to go to Boy Scouts and didn't give me the option to say no. It wasn't that I didn't want to learn skills and get merit badges, but I felt cheated out of the time I didn't get with guys who weren't alive anymore. I wanted to ride in the car with Uncle Kirk and ride horses with Uncle Clayton and play basketball with Poppa Dale. I had heard about these men and their hobbies but never got to experience them, and now they were gone. I didn't want to tie knots with some other dude who didn't have basketballs or horses or racecars.

I didn't know how to process my emotions, didn't know how to tell my dad what I was feeling, so I just cried in my room. Mom and Dad always gave me my own room, even when my dad moved us to Kanab as a family of seven on a fifteen-thousand-dollar teacher's salary to a four-bedroom trailer that cost around thirty grand. I don't know how they made it work.

Breaking away from the ranch was hard for Dad. He gave up flight school at FIT to take out a loan and try to become partners with his dad, my Grandpa Tom, and turn the ranch into a profitable business. There is no harder business than ranching. There are an infinite number of variables and no guarantees. Sometimes the cows die just because it's too cold. Or they fall in a creek. Sometimes the crops don't grow. Or they do grow, but then nobody wants to buy them. Or the barn burns down. Or disease spreads through and wipes out the crops, the cows, or both.

The ranch partnership between Dad and Grandpa Tom failed. Dad went to work on oil rigs across Canada, and then decided to move us in with his sister in British Columbia so he could go back to school to become a teacher. Then he and Mom decided to get us out of Canada.

Before we moved, Dad was my teacher. He taught me science and social studies in fourth and fifth grade. I would finish my work quickly and start making trouble, so he would send me outside to run laps around the school. If that wasn't enough, he would send me home to fill up empty milk jugs with water from the school drinking fountains. Dad had a key to the school. The house we rented was just outside the north entrance. I mowed lawns for neighbors and saved the money to pay for my Latter-day Saint mission. I also wanted to buy a PlayStation and save up to buy a car when I turned sixteen.

Ten percent of everything I earned went to the Church. I paid tithing before I bought anything else. When the book drives came to school, Mom would match the money I spent, and she helped me buy books. I read all the Tolkien books, the

Jacques books, the Narnia series, the Bible and Book of Mormon, all of John Grisham and Gary Paulsen and Orson Scott Card. I loved stories. I started writing my own. Our home did not have many bedrooms, so Mom helped me move into a tent in the unfinished basement so I could have privacy while writing and reading. Living in a tent felt like its own story to me. I felt like the main character from one of my favorite books, *My Side of the Mountain.*

I had a crush on the girl next door. She was the principal's daughter and was a couple grades older than me. She was extremely athletic. We often got caught up in excess competitiveness. At school we did as many sit-ups as we could in sixty seconds. When we played hockey in PE, I didn't care about anything but beating her. She liked to read, just like me. One of the big events at the school was the annual weekly read-a-thon culminating in a big reading sleepover in the school gym to help everyone pile on the minutes. I had to beat her. I looked at the prizes and minutes you needed to read and figured if I read just over three hours a day, Monday to Friday, I could log two thousand minutes, which was a nice even number beyond the top prize. All the minutes had to be recorded, signed by an adult, and tallied before submitting to the judges. I knew she would be thinking the same thing and probably have the same stretch goal. So, I needed to get two thousand and one.

But I also had seen *The Price Is Right.* If she was trying to beat me, which I thought she was, she would probably have these same thoughts too. I decided to go for two thousand and *two* minutes. The awards assembly came, and I went first. Two thousand and two. I looked at her face and knew I had won. She stood up a few minutes later with a tally of two thousand and one. I beat her by one minute. She could not argue that I cheated, because I went first.

The next and last stop of my childhood was in Kanab, where we landed after leaving Canada and where I started my sixth-grade year. When I picked up a basketball for the first time at a park with some kids after we moved to Kanab, everything suddenly felt better. The small school in Canada did not have team sports. I had watched sports for a few years but hadn't played any. Holding this large ball in my two hands, feeling the rubber lines between the leather, ultimately arcing it up into the air in a perfect spin through the hoop, brought a wonderful feeling. The feeling of shooting a basketball just made sense, kind of like reading or writing a story. I felt unsettled after all our moves, and now having to start over yet again. When I held a basketball I felt a sense of control. I was in charge. I could decide whether the ball went through the hoop. I could do that. Mom told me it was in my blood, that Poppa Dale was a great basketball player, and I could be, too. She played with me sometimes.

"See it going through the hoop," Mom would say. "If you can see it happening, it will happen."

As much as I wanted to enjoy the activity and have fun, I felt pressure to be great. Mom and Dad poured us a concrete pad and got me a basketball hoop that first Christmas in Kanab. I went there every day. I would get off the bus, walk home, pull the laundry in off the clothesline, play hockey on my PlayStation for half an hour, and then go play basketball outside. Or ride my bike to Tanner's house and play basketball there.

Tanner was the friend I finally made at age eleven who I had needed my whole life. We played basketball together for years, and as high school seniors won the state championship in football. Everything was better with Tanner around.

That first year in Kanab was hard for Mom and Dad. Moving a thousand miles away uncovered deep wounds. Mom had never wanted to go to Canada to begin with. They did a good job protecting us from their conversations, but the tension at home was thick. Four-seven-four West Kane Drive was a small house for a big family. It was too small for Dad, who for a short time after our move lived at the hitch'n'post a mile away. He would still come home often to see us, and when I saw him walking down Kane Drive, I would run to him and walk with him.

"Your mom needs a little space right now, and I can give her some space," said Dad as we walked. "Look what I found at the campground last night!" And then he would show me a cool rock or a small piece of old metal.

He was always picking up random objects from campgrounds and roadsides and repurposing them. My best sleeping bag to this day came from the side of the road. I wore a Mickey Mouse hat as a youngster that he spotted while driving on the freeway. He would routinely spot something, pull over, run through traffic and grab his prize, and run back, usually amid half-serious protests from my mom. His best hammer also came from the side of the road. Bailing twine, a left shoe, coolers, all sorts of things.

I was used to Dad being gone for periods of time. After a few years of working near home in Kanab, Dad hit the road again. He spent weeks and months away working in reservation schools across Arizona, and then a few years in Wisconsin before finally coming home for good.

I was grateful both my parents were there when I went to Karen's parents' house to pick up the boys.

She didn't know I was taking the boys back to Georgia. She expected me to exercise my parent time and then return them to her at her parents' house. When we finally drove up to their front lawn, I felt like a secret agent. I didn't think the exchange would work. Something would tip them off, they would try to stop me from leaving, the kids would get caught in the middle. I was jittery beyond butterflies.

I walked up to the front door like I had a million times before. Brian opened, smiled, and went to shake my hand like always. I shook his hand but didn't smile. He went over on the lawn and made small talk with my dad. The boys jumped outside, said hi to me, and ran to see my mom. I saw their luggage through the open door and quickly went to grab it. I was on a rescue mission with no time for distractions.

Karen bumped into me outside Brian's office. "Can we talk?" She touched my arm, motioning to the office. Her parents thought I wasn't strong enough to go through with the divorce. They thought I would stay with Karen for the kids, that all I needed was more of Brian's lessons. It was like a ritual; he would tell us when we needed a lesson, and we would sit with him in his office for however many hours were needed to teach us his approach to life and love. Not this time. I was so glad I didn't have to sit through any more of his psychology lessons!

I kept moving toward the boys' backpacks and said nothing. I gathered up the luggage and beelined back to the car. My mom already had the boys in their car seats. Dad peeled away from Brian, and as we sped away, I looked back to see him frowning his signature unibrow frown, arms at his sides, standing in the middle of his lawn.

I knew that so much of Karen's pain stemmed from her dad. As sad as that felt, I could not try to save her from him anymore. I had swooped in seven years ago to save her from her mean ex-boyfriends and her controlling father. I failed. I hoped that I would never have to see him again. I did hope Karen could find happiness with someone else, but did not wish that future father-in-law on anyone.

We had gone into enemy territory and completed our mission. Mission accomplished!

"Wahoo!" said Gramalisa, same as she had done when I called her with the divorce news three weeks earlier.

We went to Costco, and I rode around on the large cargo cart with the boys and ate samples. Then we went to the parking lot, and I took turns throwing them high in the air and catching them until I couldn't lift my arms. They seemed heavier since I had last seen them. Two-year-olds grow quickly, but by the time they are four like Rex, you can't recognize them after two weeks.

In between tosses they shouted, "Again! Again!" in delight. We went back to Kanab for the night before starting the long drive back to Georgia the next day. Mom decided to come with me and take whatever time off I needed. Dad would stay in Kanab. We didn't have a plan. But I had my babies back. I would be fine.

I sat in the back while Mom drove us for three days over two thousand miles. We took selfies and had tickle fights and ate an eight-pound bag of Albanese gummy bears. The second day we stopped at a McDonald's, where the boys FaceTimed their mom. We kept it short and pretended to be in Utah. Right after that my boss called.

"Dude, I have an early Christmas present for you, but what's up with your numbers this month?"

My numbers this month? Numbers . . . numbers . . . oh, shoot, I hadn't worked basically the entire month of October because of this divorce mess. Since I started, the three minority partner-owners of Imaca had wanted me to join them as a VP. I knew there was a good chance that might happen at the end of the year. I was already set to make close to two hundred thousand dollars that year, more than double what I ever had before. From what they told me about the VP job, the promotion wouldn't mean more money because of how well I was already doing, but I could make a much bigger impact. And maybe more money in the long term.

"Arron is so pissed at your numbers, he's talking about firing you. So, fix your numbers and then get that Christmas present. Okay, buddy, bye-bye."

Arron, my CEO, was as direct as they come. His anger was justified. Get fired or get promoted. I could do a lot in a few days. We'd get back to Georgia, get back to normal, Mom could stay with the kids, and I would crush work harder than ever before. Easy peasy.

The drive was long and hard in Mom's little Kia sedan. The second night we snuck into the closed indoor hotel pool, and Rex practiced throwing the water wheely life preserver at me, trying to ring me like a lassoed calf. When he finally ringed me, we laughed so hard the front desk heard us and came and kicked us out. The pool was closed, after all.

We stopped for a final meal at a Chick-fil-A just a few hours from home. It didn't feel like home anymore, and likely wouldn't be home much longer, but it was home for now. The home where Rex got his first fire ant bite and saw his first wild armadillo. The home where Rhett got his first stitches when Rex knocked his highchair over and Rhett toppled headfirst onto tile floor. The home where their mom grinned at me like she wanted to hire Satan to torture me for telling her I fell in love with another woman.

That weekend we took the boys walking for miles in their stroller, ate way too much ice cream, and took them to the drive-through wild animal park in Lagrange, Georgia. The whole park smelled like spores. Moldy, hairy, inbred, dusty, dirty spores. We bought large feed pellets for the animals. When we pulled up to the lion, the lion was laying on his raised platform, resting and swatting flies. I told Rex I thought I could wake him up with a well-aimed toss of a food pellet. I chucked the pellet out my window about twenty yards and bounced right off the lion's royal rump. The lion leapt to his feet, and Rex squealed with delight.

In an act of instant karma, a large and dirty cow reached its head through Rex's window with its mouth wide open, eagerly awaiting one of those big yummy pellets. I tossed the pellet into the cow's gaping mouth. She grappled at the pellet with her long tongue, only to launch it back out again and right into Rex's forehead like a wine cork popping off a wine bottle. It even made the noise, *pop*! Rex was already laughing at the lion, but now he really started to roar. I caught the whole thing on my phone camera. We rolled up the windows and watched the sequence on repeat during the hour-drive home.

At home, Mom taped construction paper over the windows. By Sunday, Karen knew I had the boys back in Georgia. I told her they were getting back into their routine and that she and her lawyer should get back to us to confirm court and mediation dates. She asked that I leave the cat's stuff on the curb when I left for work in the morning.

When I left my mom to take the boys to preschool, we had the uneasy feeling that our little utopia was coming to an end. The boys were happy to see their friends again, but I was sad to drop them off. I planned to pick them up early and take them across the street to Chick-fil-A. I had to work, especially with the added pressure from my boss's recent phone call. I couldn't risk getting fired just when my career was taking off.

As I drove away from the preschool, I wanted to turn back, at least for Rhett, and not work, and risk getting fired. No two-year-old wants to sit in a daycare. *This is temporary*, I told myself, *and for me to win custody of the boys, I need to get them back on their regular schedule just like Tom said.*

We never made it to Chick-fil-A that afternoon. Karen emailed me late that morning and said that she had picked up the boys. She was taking them to a new preschool closer to downtown Atlanta, that cost $3000 per month, and I had to pay for it. I drove home later, depressed, with no boys. My mom wasn't surprised. She offered to take me on a Mommy date like she had when I was growing up.

I had loved going on Mommy dates when I was younger. Being the oldest of five kids wasn't easy. It seemed like Mom was always pregnant. The first time she asked me to cook dinner I was only eight. Mom was sick on the couch, about to give birth to my younger brother Kyle, and Dad was gone at night school, so Mom walked me through how to make goulash and mashed potatoes. Our next Mommy date after that, I felt like a good son. We drank her favorite soda together, Black Cherry Shasta. She always made time to take each of us on one Mommy date per month.

Now I felt like a failed son. We rode go karts in downtown Atlanta and did our best to have some fun. On the drive home, roads everywhere were closed due to some sort of event. Two were closed, then three were closed, then four. Every way I tried to go home was closed. I got so frustrated. The drive home represented exactly how I felt. The boys were gone again, and we didn't have a mediation date or a court date, and there was no progress. October 2016 was the month that lasted a year.

In my frustration, I asked my mom to leave and go back to Utah. I needed to work, the boys were gone, she was so great to come out with me, but she might as well go home. She wanted to find some way to help me, but there was nothing any of us could do other than follow the steps and wait. She reluctantly agreed and drove off the next morning while I drove off to work. I cried most of the next day.

I usually called Nikki when I cried. By this point, she knew me better than anyone. She listened to me for hours. She liked my stories about growing up and raising cattle and playing high school sports and all of it. I was so sad and lonely, I caught myself thinking at times I might as well just go for it with Nikki. I still felt that I needed her because mediation wasn't until the end of November and our court date wasn't until the first week in December. I could not have found a more willing participant. She was such a good listener and had always had time for me. She wanted to move to Georgia with me and she wanted to come visit.

I did not think I could risk Karen finding out that I wasn't in love with Nikki. I thought if Karen found out I was not actually in love with Nikki, she would refuse to sign divorce papers. No Nikki, no divorce. Whether this was true or not I'll never know, but it's what I believed. So, with weeks to kill before I could get divorced, Nikki came to visit me in Atlanta.

As soon as I saw her come up the escalator at Hartsfield-Jackson arrivals, I knew I couldn't do it anymore. I had only seen her a couple times in person, and her flying across the country to visit helped me finally see how unfairly I was treating her. I felt disgusted with myself. As our weekend together moved along, I counted the hours until I would take her back to the airport. I needed to level with her and tell her the truth.

Dad and Kyle came to visit for Thanksgiving the next week. We played football and took the boys camping. My little Corolla was making a strange noise, but it got us into the Georgia mountains for waterfall hikes and kayak rides. We probably shouldn't have camped without blankets or swam in Tallulah Falls in November, but we survived. The boys had sleeping bags and stayed warm. This was the first time I took them camping. Karen had never allowed it. This was the good life. Court was right around the corner, and then we would be home free.

My sister Kelly joined me for our day in court. Tom had accidentally double-booked the day, so we waited in the courtroom without him most of the day. Karen and her lawyer sat on the other side. The pre-hearing mediation was short and pointless, like I knew it would be. This was the day I would get justice.

We started in the middle of the afternoon and went on until around seven p.m. Karen had a lot to say about me. She complained about my mom giving Rex an oatmeal bath and read aloud the emails I had written to Nikki. One of the emails mentioned how ridiculous Nikki's hair looked in the morning. Karen was certain that meant we had sex, and she told the judge as much. I'd never even meet Nikki outside of work until three days after Karen left with the boys, but hey, this was what I asked for. As far as me wanting Karen to believe I was having an affair, it was working. Karen concluded by saying how much she loved me and how badly she just wanted me back.

She deserved an Oscar for her performance.

Next it was my turn.

Her lawyer badgered me with a bunch of questions about the doctrine of our church and my relationship with Nikki. I didn't say much. I reaffirmed that I needed out.

Then Tom got my sister Kelly on the stand, and she testified of me working from home while being the primary caretaker for the kids at the same time. She shared that Karen was unstable and often unloving. Kelly shared a recent example of when she lived with us in the fall of 2015. She was watching the boys while Karen was out doing something else, and then Karen came home. My sister had dressed them, fed them, taken care of them for the day, and was now playing with them.

"Aw, they look so cute," Karen had said. "Here, take my phone and get a picture of us for my Instagram."

She had my sister take as many pictures as it took to get "the right" one and then abruptly left. This was a perfect example of how Karen operated. None of the work, all the glory. She wanted people to like her and think she was a good mom while at the same time she hated mothering. She wanted people to think she was a good Latter-day Saint while at the same time hating the church. Tom then backed up my sister's testimony with the dozens of affidavits I gathered from friends and family.

Then Karen's lawyer took her turn at my sister. I have never felt more helpless. The job of a big brother is to take care of his siblings. I failed miserably that day in court. I sat watching the verbal blood bath in front of me.

"Isn't it true that you are openly gay in a church that doesn't allow homosexuals?"

"Isn't it true that you are a drug addict and an alcoholic?"

"Isn't it true that your issues with your parents are so bad you have been kicked out of your own home many times, and that's the only reason you lived with my client?"

"Isn't it true that you have failed out of multiple colleges because your drug abuse has rendered you incompetent?"

Eventually she stopped. Kelly was broken. I was too. I couldn't believe I let her come and support me in such an emotionally dangerous situation. I should have known this would happen. I glanced over, and even my almost-ex-wife looked ashamed. It was the most vicious attack I had ever seen.

The judge came back and gave Karen primary custody and had me pay exactly what Tom had me offer her in the beginning, three months earlier. It's based on an income worksheet. Karen had earned nothing, and I had earned 100% of our income. The fact that I helped get her through two and a half degrees didn't matter, the text messages I provided where she said, "I can't be alone with these kids!" and "Take me away from your offspring!" didn't matter. She was the mom, and I was the money.

And then it was done. We would meet in a few months to turn this temporary order into a final judgment of divorce.

"Now he can go be with Nikki," I heard Karen say. She would not keep trying to win me back, because she believed I was in love with someone else. I was free, but at what cost?

She could take the money. She could take whatever she wanted. But I would no longer give her the power to hurt the people I loved. I did my worst, and now she had done hers.

We were done.

Chapter 2

April Showers and Mayflowers

YOU TOLD ME IT WAS REAL, AND I SAID I DIDN'T believe you, and then you told me it was real again!" Nikki cried above her noodle bowl the weekend after the hearing. I was back in Utah for the work Christmas party where I spent the previous night dodging her. Now we shared a booth at a hole-in-the-wall noodle spot across the street from her condo.

"I know, and I am so sorry," I said. "I'll never forget how you were there for me. But this is over."

"Was it real, or not?" she accused me through her tears. "Did you just make everything up? I knew I was just a phase for you!" She loved that word, phase. In the beginning, in the love emails we wrote, she often called herself a phase. Women always know.

"I don't know," I said. "I was going through a lot, but it's mostly over now, and I can't do this anymore."

"So, you only needed me to help you with your divorce, and now you're done with me?"

"I appreciate the time we shared," I responded, "but I'm not in a position to share any more time together."

Our CEO brought me in the next morning and announced my promotion to VP. I would fly to a lot of cities and hire a lot of people, which would keep me out of Atlanta in my downtime. I needed that. Being home was hard. Being away sounded perfect. I might make less money in 2017 than I would if I didn't take the promotion, because I was so good at the sales position itself, but the two-to-three-year payoff looked good. And the salary portion was higher, which would help with the new condo I wanted to purchase in the city near where Karen had moved with the boys.

More work, less money, less time to wallow in my misery. Deal.

I figured I had about three years of difficult times ahead before things normalized. That's basically how alimony works in Georgia. I don't know why I had to pay alimony, but I did, and it lasts about half the time you were married. Since we were married six years, I would pay alimony for three. I also had a student loan to pay off and a few years of the expensive inner-city daycare Karen found for the boys. I had to make it through the next three years, and then I would start over. I read books on trauma and divorce, and they all said healing takes time.

Staying busy hiring and traveling for work would get me through those years faster. I sent the promotion details to my mortgage officer, who reminded me of the risks of buying a home while in the middle of a divorce. So, I got creative.

I looked up the schools in Karen's neighborhood: worst test scores in the state. Literacy rate under fifty percent. Strange dress code rules. Warnings and advisories that disguised crime and drugs into opportunities for the kids to work on community improvement projects. Rex would start kindergarten in the fall. This couldn't happen. I raised my concerns to Karen, and she emailed me the school district homepage with a graffiti project the kids from different backgrounds would do together to be inclusive.

I called her. "Karen, starting Rex in school down there is a terrible idea," I said. "You are a smart person, and you value education enough to be going for a PhD. This would be a terrible mistake, and we are not going to do it."

"Okay, you're right," she said.

What? I said she had a terrible idea, and she admitted it? This had never happened before. I had been such a pushover when we were married. Now that I was finally speaking up, I might over-correct, but at least it had worked this time.

"Okay, great," I said. "I'll get a place nearby with the best schools in Atlanta. I already have some options."

And I did. But we were still married. Any property I purchased while married was considered "marital property," and half belonged to Karen. I didn't clarify what I meant by "get a place" and she never asked. I had my dad co-sign on the mortgage application to safeguard the purchase. As long as it was in both mine and my dad's name, I could argue that it wasn't *my* property, which meant it wasn't *marital* property. I had no idea if that argument would hold up in court if it came to that, but it seemed plausible.

I gave Karen too much credit. She never asked whether I bought my place and never pursued it as possible marital property. She never brought it up at all.

I found a condo in the best school district in Fulton County. I had a large commission check coming from December, always our best month of the year. Starting in January, my salary would increase, but I wouldn't have any commission checks for several months. I underestimated how much this would pinch my payments to Karen, disrupt my condo purchase, and strain my ability to pay my lawyer.

I signed the final mortgage documents on Friday, January 13, 2017.

This was the first proactive thing I had done in my adult life. I was making my own choices without looking for someone to please.

Thanks to my move, Rex would start an excellent kindergarten that fall. I was about to turn twenty-eight. Although the past year had felt impossibly hard, and the next three years were shaping up to be difficult, I was ready for the challenge. I told my parents and Kelly that we needed to hike the Grand Canyon rim-to-rim when my birthday came around on May 11. They agreed.

Waiting out the temporary order until we could get our final divorce judgment seemed to take forever. Every week or two, I would have Tom tweak some things and shoot it over to Karen and Anne. Every time they asked for more. There was no specific timeline for when the divorce would go through. I still wondered if Karen would somehow learn I was not in a relationship with Nikki. We were in a mystery mandatory waiting period that seemed to have no end.

Months dragged by. The limbo state of being separated-not-divorced kept all my misdeeds fresh on my mind. I felt guilty and judged myself harshly. I thought back on the term the judge used when determining to grant a divorce: "irreparable harm." I had caused that. Even though I often shifted the blame onto Karen, in my silent moments I felt terrible.

All my prior year savings went toward the down payment on my condo and paying my lawyer fees, which were right around $20k, just like my friend Scott said they'd be. I had nothing left. I started using coupons for the first time in my life.

I saved everywhere I could. I bought no furniture. Instead of chairs I bought cheap plastic wiggle cars for us to ride around on, turning the hardwood floor into a racetrack. Instead of sofas, I bought a giant used bean bag. I found the boys a bunkbed on Craigslist. I lived in an affluent area and was amazed at the high-quality stuff the homeowners around me sold for practically nothing. I felt like Templeton from Charlotte's Web "when the lights go out." I added a Craigslist bounce house with a ball pit for Rhett's birthday on March 11, 2017, to complete the furnishings in the condo. When I was on my mission in Oregon years earlier, we visited a home where they had converted a large in-home wine cellar at the end of a hallway into a ball pit. I vowed to make one in my home one day. Until then, the bounce house would have to do.

I still operated on a deficit and was unable to save anything. I decided to occupy the great room and posted my bedroom on Craigslist. By the end of the month, I had a tenant on a one-year contract.

As I went through my clothes and possessions, I realized that many brought up painful memories. I donated and recycled and sent things down the 7th-story trash chute in the hallway. I kept thinning things out until I had only three small possessions left from my marriage.

The first to go was a rare antique vase we purchased from a shop in Park City, Utah, early in the marriage. I remembered the cold and blustery night we stepped into one of the many cozy and artistic little shops to see what unique and duly overpriced treasures lay on the shelves inside. It was made of a concrete alloy that looked like petrified wood. We had filled it with matching artisanal cinnamon-stick flowers that were still pungent all these years later. I have a scar on my wrist that looks the same as the pattern on the vase. I suddenly hated it.

The second was a snake carving I got in Bali where I thought Karen contracted dengue fever and would die. As a possession from my married days, I should get rid of it; as a representation of my defiance and resilience to survive tough times, I should keep it. I needed a few days to decide.

The snake eyes followed me around the condo. They watched me while I slept on the fold-out love seat. "What will you do?" the snake eyes asked me. "Will you toss me down the trash chute?"

The third was a mounted fish Karen's grandpa made for me when I caught the whopper with him near Fish Lake in Utah. I made a video recording of the catch on my phone and her grandpa had me play it for him several times. It was huge, twenty-two inches long. In life it had weighed three or four pounds and was now mounted to a nice piece of driftwood with moss.

I loved Karen's grandpa. In my opinion he was the most sensible person in her family. We had gone hunting and fishing and shooting. He called me several times during the months of our separation. I never answered because part of me didn't want to get divorced from his granddaughter because I feared it would break his heart. I hadn't had a grandpa in my life since I was very young. Karen's grandpa had been my grandpa.

I simmered on thoughts of what to do with the vase, snake, and fish for several days. Finally, I determined that I needed them gone. I rounded up the boys and told them we needed to throw the fish down the trash chute. Rex thought the fish was creepy, so he was all for it. I had him toss the fish. Then I had Rhett toss the snake. Then I tossed the vase. It turned into a game. We ran back and forth from the condo to the trash chute, finding whatever waste we could, opening the hatch and tossing them into the abyss. Old toys, old socks, whatever we could find, we just kept tossing. It felt good. Tossing whatever we wanted down the ancient echoing chambers of a seventh-story trash chute felt like an important step in the healing process.

After the boys fell asleep, a signature Atlanta downpour filled the sky. I walked outside by the condo pool that wouldn't open for two months and screamed into the inky black night sky. I rain-danced and screamed until I fell to my knees crying and praying I could move on. I needed God to keep breaking me down to the bottom of who I was so I could find myself. I felt like I had become a shell of myself, nothing but one coping mechanism on top of another coping mechanism. The real Matt was way, way down there somewhere, gone for a long time. I was determined to find myself. That night I prayed to God to break me down so I could find Him.

And He did.

Over the next six weeks, everything around me fell apart.

I finished my taxes for the year and found I owed the IRS over nine thousand dollars.

Then my car died. It had been acting funny for months and the check-engine light had been on for over a year, but I always had a friend who could shut it off. Not anymore. My friend replaced the spark plugs and coil somethings, and then I rear-ended a kid on my way out of his shop. Pure brain-body malfunction. I hadn't been sleeping well from the months-long stress of getting divorced, and when I told my foot to hit the brakes, it hit the gas instead.

That day I realized I wasn't in control of myself. I needed to cool off. My brain failed to tell my foot to hit the brakes, and I slammed the kid good from behind while he was at a full stop. He called insurance and received an injury settlement, and my monthly premiums skyrocketed.

My car wouldn't pass inspections and sometimes it died, but for the most part it would at least fire up and go. I took it into a shop and found it was only firing on three of the four cylinders.

It would not pass inspections no matter what, and it could die any day. My options were to spend three thousand dollars on a new engine or buy a new car.

I walked out of the lobby and fell to my knees in the parking lot. I closed my eyes and just knelt there until I could think. And then I prayed.

"Heavenly Father, keep my car going until I am back on my feet. I have no other choice. Keep my car alive."

I opened my eyes and immediately saw things differently. That day my eyes changed. My outlook changed. I was full of confidence. I believed God had my back. As bad as things seemed, it was better than before. I was free. I could breathe again. I could laugh. My head and my chest didn't hurt anymore. My entire marriage had been full of stress and anxiety. I felt like a brand-new man. As long as I could feel the air in my lungs, I was better off than before. Whether my car died or not, I was good.

It took lots of intention to come back to that place of personal power. I would get distracted and downtrodden and frustrated for the next two or three years. And especially over the next two months. But God kept sprinkling my life with little bright spots of absolute clarity that gave me what I needed.

Another one came when I taught Rex how to ride a bike on the elementary school track a couple blocks south from our condo. He was turning five and hadn't ridden a bike without training wheels. We were working toward it the previous summer when divorce got me distracted. I went to my favorite upscale thrift store and got him a killer bike with sixteen-inch wheels. It was chrome and aluminum with hand brakes.

Like most things, Rex picked up riding without training wheels in one day. He fell several times, but soon flew around the quarter-mile track at the elementary school like it was nothing.

He passed me taking a video of him with my phone and shouted out his customary, "Daddy, send that to Auntie Kelly!"

Later that week, he rode down a hill for the first time and felt that magical weightless feeling of coasting in low gravity on a bicycle. He thought he had learned to fly.

"Daddy, I feel the wind!" he exclaimed in pure ecstasy. "I feel the wind!"

Later he explained. "Dad, birds have hollow bones and that's how they can fly, and when I rode down the hill, I felt the wind in my bones, and I thought I could fly too!"

I knew the best thing I could be was a dad.

Just like I knew my car would not die. My dad wanted to buy me a new one. I refused. I needed things around me to run their course. I told him as Nikki had run her course, this little car needed to run its course. I would drive it unregistered.

Karen and I agreed I would up the ratio of child support to alimony so she could keep more money for a longer time period without paying as much in taxes, and in exchange she would cover the boys' health insurance while she was in school because it was basically free. A win-win to seal the deal. We had finally reached an agreement.

We decided to meet in a few days, the first weekend of April, to sign the divorce decree. I told Tom I was signing it. He told me not to. I told him to take a hike and that all he wanted was to bill me for more hours. We were on the phone for maybe four minutes.

He billed me for that last phone call.

When I signed the divorce papers on April 6th, I noticed that her lawyer added that I had to pay Karen's lawyer fees, around eight thousand dollars. I wasn't surprised. I paused and clicked the pen a few times, wondering if I should still sign. I knew Tom would say not to, but I just wanted to be done with this. I had no money to pay Karen's lawyer and didn't know when I would have the money.

I signed. Within a day or two I received an email of our Decree signed by all parties. I was finally divorced! A huge burden fell from my shoulders.

I decided to be proactive about the lawyer fees and emailed her lawyer. "Anne," I wrote, "I am unable to pay you. My finances are completely depleted. What do we do now?"

She replied, "I can garnish your wages if you agree to it, or we can go back to court."

I had options! How nice!

I responded, "If my wages are garnished, I won't be able to pay my child support, alimony, and the new childcare bill. I suppose we will need to go back to court. Let me know."

I never heard back from Anne. I worried she might serve me with court papers, but soon I stopped worrying. I left the worries behind. I had completed the divorce process and felt like I could do anything.

I felt equally electric and elated and, at the same time, sad and alone. For nearly seven years I had been the guardian, protector, defender, and slave to a controlling woman. I gave up my friends, my faith, my hobbies, my family, and myself to take care of her. Now she was gone forever.

I didn't know the extent of it yet, but she had become my full identity. Now that she was gone, I had very little left. I was empty. That's a tricky spot to be in. So, I prayed. Just like when my car died. I prayed and prayed until I started to hear the voice of God again. It took a long time.

Karen would have primary legal and physical custody. That's how they do it in Georgia. I knew she hated parenting, but she wanted the money and the image of keeping primary custody. The standard arrangement for dads in Georgia is one weeknight a week and every-other-weekend. I wanted more time with my boys. She agreed to every other Wednesday through Monday. That would be enough. It would be almost impossible to balance with my work travel schedule, but the boys were more important. I would find a way to parent them during their most formative years. I didn't trust their mom to do it.

I mapped out my debts and commitments in my journal. Three years of alimony, three years of expensive daycare, one student loan to pay off, and a lot of trauma to heal from. In 2020, three years from now, things would become easier. By 2020, I determined, I would feel like myself again.

I could live with that.

I turned that page of my journal into my vision board of where I would be in 2020. I looked at it daily. Loans paid, alimony paid, wounds healed, money in the bank, ready for a new relationship. The next three years would be all I needed to get back on track.

The day after our divorce, I went to Karen's apartment to pick up the boys. In an honest moment as she walked past me, she broke down and cried and came in for a hug. She had lost a lot of weight as I had. She asked me to come in and fix her vacuum. I politely declined. I wrote in my journal that night, "She cried a little tonight . . . I cried for seven years trying to make it work."

In those seven years, everything about me had atrophied, crusted over, and died. My writing skills, my athletic ability, my confidence. Even my love of shoes, these signature things that made me "me." I decided to bring it all back.

It was hard. I journaled every night. My cursive writing was horrible. I can barely read those first few months of journal entries. I started a blog called *lonelychristian*. I wrote a new post every night. I started reading again, one book a week, sometimes more, like I used to. I called at least one family member every day to tell them I loved them. I planned a lot of camping trips and fun outings for the boys and me.

The weekend of my divorce, my best friend came back to visit. Auntie Kelly. Just like during my marriage, Auntie Kelly was never far away. We played with the boys and went to a Hawks basketball game and bought new hiking shoes from REI for our Rim-to-Rim Grand Canyon hike coming up for my birthday the following month. I always felt better with my sister Kelly around.

My favorite history author Nathaniel Philbrick was coming to town on May 11, my birthday. I was torn about whether I should attend his lecture. Starting to do the things I loved again was a big part of my healing journey, and I wanted to do something fun for my birthday. My condo I bought in Buckhead was conveniently located next to the Atlanta History Center, where I had started going to lectures on Tuesdays. History and writing were two of my biggest hobbies before I ditched them for watching Kardashians at night with Karen. Now, I read Philbrick's books again. *The Mayflower, Bunker Hill, In the Heart of the Sea,* and one of his latest and probably my favorite, *Valiant Ambition.* I imagined myself asking him questions, having a two-way conversation with the most prolific history author of my lifetime.

As fun as the lecture would be, I had bigger things on my mind. Rex had been acting out at preschool. Pulling down his pants, saying swear words, interrupting the teacher. I needed to spend more time with him. A long birthday weekend could be the perfect option. Since we moved to Georgia a year and a half ago, he had been in too much daycare and preschool, and

I feared he wasn't getting the love and attention he needed. We went to a sawmill and bought a slab of wood. In the evenings after Rhett fell asleep, Rex and I turned the raw slab into our dining room table. I had three years to recover from my marriage, and that meant spending a lot of time with the boys, who needed healing as much as I did. I decided to do as many things as I could with Rex, who was now five; and for Rhett, who just turned three, to find more time to sit and hold him and read to him. I had held him and read to him very little in his first three years. The next three would be different.

To help decide what to do for my birthday, I went back to the vision board in my journal. It showed a divorce payoff timeline that ended with Rex turning eight in February 2020. Three expensive years ahead, financially and emotionally. I looked at the priorities I had drawn up. *Pay debts, heal wounds, save money, ready for a new relationship.* With a clear vision ahead of me, I needed to stay the course.

Rex was passionately and fully into dinosaurs: drawing them, building them, imagining them. I found the biggest interactive dinosaur theme park in North America, Kings Island in Ohio. It was only a seven-hour drive. I decided to take the Thursday-Friday of my birthday off to take Rex there for a few days. Philbrick would have to lecture without me.

I got the tickets and showed Rex where we were going.

"Wait, what?" Rex screamed in delight, looking up at me. "Can we move there?"

"I don't know if we can move there," I chuckled, "but we can play there for two days straight!"

I rented us a car for the drive from Atlanta to Ohio. My half-broken car was for local driving only. We drove the rental to Kings Island theme park just outside Cincinnati. Every night in the hotel, we watched Rex's favorite movie, *Jurassic Park,* the original. The interactive dinosaur exhibit was closed, so we snuck under the "closed" ropes. Rex climbed on the dinosaurs and rode them. When we saw maintenance workers, we ran around them and hid in bushes and hopped fences. We ate two or three carrot cakes and fifteen-dollar chocolate bars and watched *Jurassic Park* again and again.

The park being closed was the best possible scenario. Normally it would have been crawling with people making sounds and smells and noise. Normally it would have taken forever for Rex to push the interactive buttons that made the dinosaurs romp and roar. But that day, my birthday, was not a normal day at the dinosaur exhibit on Kings Island. There were zero spectators, and the only sound was Rex reading the dino bios and squealing with delight when he recognized a species, like his favorite "Spinosaurus." There was zero safety or security personnel. Rex rode every animal he wanted to ride, even when I had to hoist him up onto some of them. He pushed every "move and roar" button, read about every plant and animal, and had the time of his life. Near the end, we came up on the "long necks," where engineers were working on a gigantic Brachiosaurus. It seemed we finally discovered why the entire exhibit was marked "closed."

"Brachio," Rex announced nonchalantly as he sized up the huge, motorized rubber replica. We quietly walked past and did not attract their attention as we left the exhibit.

That night we had dinner at Buffalo Wild Wings. Before dinner, Rex neatly unfolded the paper cuff around the napkin that held his utensils. He wrote with the crayons in the kids' pack they provided him. "I love you, Dad." He handed it to me and kept drawing.

I wept while he drew. I kept the napkin note in my journal. I still felt like a failed parent. His note helped.

That night at the hotel we celebrated my birthday by watching *Jurassic Park* twice. We ate an entire carrot cake between the two of us while we enjoyed Rex's favorite movie and jumped back and forth between our queen-sized beds. Rex finally fell asleep after I started the movie a third time.

Our second day at the park Rex felt like he owned the place. "Hi, this is my dad Matt, and my name is Rex, and I'm a genius," he said and then casually walked away.

While in Ohio, we talked about Rex's upcoming kindergarten and how he would ride the bus and make new friends. He was graduating from preschool and moving on in life. We had already visited the school and Rex was extremely excited. Rhett, on the other hand, had two more years of preschool left. Karen wanted Rhett to stay in preschool alone through the summer.

"Rex, your mom wants Rhett to stay in school this summer," I told Rex.

"I know, Dad. He hates it. I wish he could go to Morris Brandon with me," Rex said.

"What if they would let you do summer school with Rhett? Would you do it?"

"And go to school with Rhett?" he asked me. "Sure, Dad! I will do it. And then next year he can come to school with me."

My heart melted at the love my son had for his brother. I emailed the preschool dean, and he approved it. Rex and Rhett would be in summer school together. I would get them out of there as often and as long as I could, but while Rhett was there the next few months, at least he would have his brother. It was expensive, but worth it. You can't put a price on spending time with your brother.

Starting that May and going through the next spring, I found one day a week to stay home with Rhett. Mostly we read books. He loved being read to. He also loved to cuddle. For about an hour each morning, the first order of business was to mess with Rex's Legos and toys and jump on his bed. Then we would restore everything to its proper place and move on with our reading. I loved holding him on my lap and reading to him. I had spent hours doing this with Rex. I didn't have as much of a chance with Rhett. I was doing my MBA when he was born, and then out working full-time a few months after I graduated. I felt like I had let him down. I was making up for lost time the best I could.

Usually while we read together, tears would stream down my cheeks. Tears of sadness because I felt like Rhett had been neglected as an infant and toddler and would likely have permanent psychological problems because of it. But also tears of gratitude that at least now I could spend one-on-one time with him. I couldn't believe I married someone who didn't want to spend mom time with such a perfect boy. I emailed her several times asking for full custody until she finished school. She refused. So, I held Rhett and I cried.

When Rex and I got back to Georgia from the dinosaur park, my dad came to town for a couple days. We played baseball together. We had our customary daily summer pool party barbecues. The pool was open at my condo from May to September, and every day we spent together, we swam and barbecued after school and work. The grills had gas lines built into them, so it was the perfect setup.

Since my tenant had the bedroom, Dad joined me in the living room on a large sofa I had added to our short list of furnishings. I didn't have very good drapes and the city lights around us woke him soon after he fell asleep.

"Time to close down the fog lights from the wharf," he muttered. "It's brighter than a dang ballroom in here!"

He's extremely talented at mixing metaphors to make memorable one-liners. I draped some blankets over the windows the best I could, and we both fell asleep.

After we took Dad to the airport on Sunday, I took the boys aside in the living room and gave them priesthood blessings. It's a thing in our church. We believe Jesus wants to heal us from sickness, comfort us when in need, and give us guidance. He does that through fathers blessing their children and leaders blessing their constituents. We put our hands on their head, call them by their full name, invoke the authority of God, and speak words of healing and guidance. It's an intimate experience for dads and their kids. When I was done, Rex asked if he could give me a blessing in return.

"Dad, can I give you one?" he asked. "I promise Jesus won't be mad."

Before he got a chance, Rhett jumped up and put his hands on my head.

"Dad, I bless you that you will climb tall mountains and even walk on the clouds. Amen."

Short and sweet. Then Rex walked over, and Rhett backed up.

"Matthew Holt Livingston," Rex announced officially and lovingly, "I bless you that you will be a very good daddy. You will have enough money to buy me lots more Legos and still pay your tithing. In the name of Jesus Christ, Amen."

I held myself together as we finished their bedtime routine, but after the boys went to bed, I wept like a child. I felt so lucky to have these beautiful boys who had me and each other. I believed we could make it through anything together.

One morning, I walked out of my bedroom to see Rex reading a bird book to Rhett, explaining the mysteries of the world to him. We read books and hiked mountains and rode horses and did everything we could in the time I could get with them. I had nothing to do on the weekends and often took them for one of Karen's weekend days. Her new boyfriend, Ron, was often there at exchanges. She had only been dating him a short while, but the boys already referred to us as "Matt Dad" and "Ron Dad."

I was having a really hard time letting love flow back into my life. It was hard for me to say "I love you" to anyone except my boys because I felt like a fraud. Most of all, I knew I didn't truly love myself. I judged and hated myself. I felt terrible that my boys had to have divorced parents. I looked back at my vision board in my journal and thought, *give it time.*

I had my own house now, where I was finally creating my own life. It was a start.

Chapter 3

Liverty

M Y SMILES LOOKED EMPTY IN OUR PICTURES THE day we hiked the Grand Canyon. It would be a long time before I could smile again. Auntie Kelly and Gramalisa and PJ hiked it with me, the entire thing, rim to rim, twenty-four miles, seven a.m. until seven p.m. It's one of the most challenging day hikes in North America. You hike about four miles down, sixteen miles across the bottom of the canyon, and then about four miles back up the other side. Other than the perilous hike-through, the only way around the Canyon is a four-hour car drive. To get back to your car, you need to either hike all the way back through or get a shuttle ride. Our plan was to park at the North Rim, hike to the South Rim and sleep in a hotel, and shuttle back to our car the next day.

We started our hike down from our drop-off point at the North Rim on opening day, May 15. We were among the first hikers on the trail. There's a half-way point with a country store and horse stables called Phantom Ranch. Dad really wanted to get to that ranch. He had done some training for the hike, but was working from his desk a lot and driving a lot, so his legs were a little strained and cramped. Every mile or so he would call out,

"Just another mile or two to Phantom Ranch!" and every time a mile or two would pass, he would call it out again. Then we passed through a little gorge into a clearing where he saw a rock formation he particularly liked and called out, "Look at that Unit!" We have since called out Units at many family gatherings. Anything new or noteworthy could be a Unit if you choose to call it so.

I wanted to enjoy the hike, to take my shirt off and jump in the water at Phantom Ranch like I normally would, to skip along the trail and jump off everything like my lighthearted self. But I felt and looked like a deer in the headlights. I was driving a broken car and living with broken finances. My life was in shambles. I was now a father of divorced kids. I was prepared for this, but it still sucked. The stories I told myself were about finding a way to survive the hike and then to survive the next three years. The hike wasn't that hard. I had good hiking shoes.

For Mom and Dad, however, the hike was brutal. Mom had a bad ankle, and Dad had a bad calf. By the time we finished the ascent to the South Rim, Dad was tapped out.

While we sat at dinner, he poured out several near-death experiences he had experienced as a kid on the ranch in Alberta, Canada. I had not seen this version of Dad before, in touch with his emotions, being vulnerable and crying and telling us stories.

On the ranch, he and his brother Clayton started driving trucks around age eight. Tractors even earlier. Young Dad was backing the truck up to a Quonset hut with Clayton backing him. Dad backed up a little too far and ended up pinning Clayton between the lowered tailgate and the hut. He knew if he put it into gear, it would likely lurch a little bit, perhaps backwards, and possibly sever his brother in half. He didn't know whether Clayton could breathe. He didn't think Clayton could survive long, so he ran and got help, and they freed him from the painful pinch where he was held.

That and several other stories came pouring out of Dad. I realized I didn't know my dad very well. My income was starting to grow, especially now that I was renting out my bedroom, and I knew I would have enough extra money to start traveling by the end of the year. I asked Dad to go to Scotland with me the following January. He agreed with no hesitation. I had a lot of healing to do in the next three years, and a big chunk of that needed to be with my parents. We decided to build a fence that summer at the house in Kanab. I sent word to all the siblings that we needed to find a way to be there for Mom's birthday in September. I had my loved ones back, and I would no longer take them for granted.

Kelly and I were only a month removed from our biggest adventure yet: New York City with Rex. I had tons of hotel and airline points from work travel, so our main expense would be food. While we hiked, we talked about the fun we would have, and all the places we would go. This helped distract me from the misery of real life. Rex was such an adventurous kid; we both knew it would be an adventure he would never forget.

I pictured Rex and me on my rollerblades and Kelly on her skateboard all over Central Park, visiting the Statue of Liberty, running away from cops and security guards, putting him in novel situations and watching how he would respond. Karen agreed to let him go. I was surprised she said yes so easily. I had stopped calling her Karen and just called her "the boys' mom." It reminded me to speak well of her and make sure the boys had a good a relationship with her.

She called me the devil. When I was FaceTiming Rex on her phone, he somehow accidentally sent me a screenshot. It had my name at the top, "Matt Dad," with the iPhone devil emoji to the left of my name and to the right of my name. I bet she didn't have a devil emoji next to the guy they called "Ron Dad." What was Karen doing telling the boys I was the devil? How badly did she speak of me around them? I reminded myself I signed up for this when I got divorced.

If ever I wanted to take Rex or Rhett or both for something out-of-state, as long as I asked to take them on one of Karen's weeks, she agreed. Rex and I did the Kings Island dinosaur park on a Karen-weekend. The New York City trip was during a Karen-week and weekend. I would often have them every weekend in a month. We would plan and she would say, "Well, that means you have them five weekends straight, are you sure?" Of course, I was sure. I wanted to be with my boys. I hoped that if I kept our calendars saved, I could become the primary custodian one day, since I spent the most time with the boys.

I did more work to save money. I got MetroPCS to save on my cell phone bill. I would live without TV and Internet. I stripped my car insurance down to the bare minimum and negotiated a great deal on renter's insurance. I used my *per diem* work money for food to buy groceries instead of meals. I shopped at Goodwill and other thrift stores, always prioritizing thrift stores in more affluent areas. I would find things new with tags for pennies on the dollar. I got the boys' bikes from there, got our tents and camping equipment from there, and got my best sport coat for work. I received compliments on it all the time. Not bad for a five-dollar purchase.

While driving the hour to my favorite thrift store the day before our summer trip to New York, I finally got pulled over in my unregistered car. He gave me a ticket, which was surprisingly small. I took the ticket with a smile, as that was my cost of doing business until my car puttered out and I had to buy a new one. I got only one more ticket like that in the next twelve months. I would pay my "unregistered vehicle" fines and keep on driving the little Corolla until the wheels fell off.

When I arrived, I quickly found an almost new "I Love New York" shirt in Rex's size. It was a sign. Our trip would be the trip of a lifetime.

When you see the events leading up to an impending injury or death, your body goes into shock. Pupils dilate and blood rushes back to your heart, making your hands and feet numb, and your heart rate accelerates to accommodate the extra blood. The worst of these shocks I had ever felt happened in Central Park on our first day in New York City.

Kelly was taking a turn with Rex sitting between her legs on the skateboard when we hit the big hill on the southeast side of the park loop heading south. We were going the opposite direction of all the other foot and bike traffic. I was riding on my rollerblades behind them, filming them on my iPhone, hoping to get some killer footage. When it was just Kelly and me, we rode fast on our boards and blades. We crashed and bailed plenty. Normally, if Kelly got going too fast, she would jump off and bail. Today she had Rex, so bailing wasn't an option. She was going way too fast. I routinely hit thirty miles per hour on my rollerblades, but I would never do that with Rex on my shoulders. We rode into this hill without having any idea of the incline ahead.

We had never been to Central Park and did not know the grade of the giant hill going south on the east side of the park. It made sense why everyone else was going the other direction. We started flying, the raucous roar of our wheels on the pavement and vicious speed catching the attention of other Central

Parkers. I would guess we hit thirty-five miles per hour. Kelly was in front of me, and the hill became steeper the farther around the bend we went. Her skateboard fell into a fit of jarring speed wobbles. Worse than I had ever seen without her trying to bail. She had Rex holding onto her front leg sitting on her board.

The wobbles became more violent, and I knew they were going to wreck. It was going to be bad. With speed wobbles, unless you slow down, there isn't much you can do. Eventually you wobble out of control and fly off your skateboard. A gaping black hole formed in my stomach as I watched them from behind. There was a rock face on one side of them and a thick line of cyclists going the opposite direction on the other. Neither Auntie Kelly nor Rex had a helmet on. I tried to drown out the black hole in my stomach with a loud silent prayer as I watched my sister and her favorite nephew shake and wobble, zooming toward their doom.

Kelly did something I did not expect. She crouched lower, reaching even higher speeds, while at the same time gaining control. I had never seen this before. I was mesmerized. I could see her carefully inhaling and exhaling by the way she moved her arms like eagle wings, and as they roared on even faster, she stabilized. As she speedily exited the wobbles she hit a large dead tree branch, probably half an inch in diameter, and it snapped in two. One half hit a cyclist in the head hard enough that he gave an audible "hey!" and the other half careened past my head.

She was now cutting down the pavement as smoothly as a surfer on a wave. Rex was holding on tight like always, and didn't move an inch left or right. By some miracle, they rode it out, and eventually we all slowed to a stop.

"Holy crap! Matt! Did you see that? Heck yeah! Whooooo! Those were the worst speed wobbles I've ever had, and we rode it out!" Kelly exclaimed, amazed at her feat, white as a ghost, the X Games champion of Central Park.

"You snapped a branch this big around!" I yelled back, also white as a ghost, and made an OK-signal sized circle with my thumb and index finger to show her the size of the branch.

Maybe the branch wasn't that big, but it sure seemed like it.

"Auntie Kelly, again, again!" yelled Rex, who had just had the ride of his life.

We looked around us and had eyeballs coming in from every direction. One guy on a longboard clapped as he rode by.

That would be a theme for the week. There are not a ton of skateboarders in New York, and not a ton of rollerbladers, either. And none of them carried a child on their shoulders or between their legs.

"Jesus take me now!" an onlooker shouted. "I seen today what I never seen before."

Rollerblading with someone on your shoulders isn't very hard. But skateboarding with a small human draped around your front foot is *difficult*. I can't do it. I have never seen another human do it. Kelly not only did it, she did it with as much speed and grace as any other ride, and she loved it. The year before when she came to visit, she took Rex twenty miles a day on golf cart paths. We spent five days in NYC and went an average of twenty-three miles a day.

"I'm turning twenty-five next month, and of everything I have ever done, this is my favorite thing in the world," said Auntie Kelly of skateboarding with Rex.

Visiting New York is not easy. It is crowded and expensive. You need plans and backup plans, a good amount of extra money, you have to be flexible, and you have to follow your gut. It's kind of like visiting a different planet with its own laws and its own species of people and its own prices for everything. Your flight will most likely be delayed because the weather is finicky. You will probably run out of money because everything costs two to three times what it does in most cities. You'll get peddled or swindled at least once. But once you get through all that, it has the greatest sights and ambiance and history and diversity of any city in America.

Before we went, I memorized every bus route and subway station between our two home bases and the places we wanted to go. I quizzed myself at night until I had it down. When you're traveling on foot, this is vital. You don't have the time to sit down and check your phone and look at maps. You want to know where the food is, where the adventure is, how far you are from home, and where you are from Central Park. I have a natural orientation for adventure, so we never got lost and never got stuck in a sketchy place after dark.

Except when we first arrived at LaGuardia Airport.

For Kelly, that was sketchy as could be.

Rex and I arrived in New York a few hours before Kelly. As our flight descended toward the city, and Rex glimpsed the fabled Statue of Liberty through his window, he exclaimed, "Daddy look, it's the Statue of Liverty!" I did not correct him. I liked the way he said it.

Kelly's layover in Detroit was delayed. Rex and I hopped on the bus to our Airbnb in Harlem where we stayed the first three nights. We would stay in Times Square the last two nights, and this little apartment at the North end of Central Park helped even out the cost of the trip. We got off the bus around ten p.m. and rollerbladed ten blocks or so to the place. I had Rex on my shoulders and our large duffel on my back, and we rode into the night. Lots of people whooped at us and we whooped right back.

Around midnight after Rex was fast asleep, Auntie Kelly called. She had finally landed. I gave her the bus instructions, the same ones that worked well for Rex and me hours earlier, but she wasn't feeling it. It was late and dark and creepy guys were everywhere. I had to go and get her. I smart-locked the door to the apartment and prayed Rex wouldn't wake up.

The street had come to life in the three hours since Rex and I had gone inside. For the first time in my life, I saw what they refer to as a "corner." People huddled close, speaking in whispers, exchanging drugs and money and secrets. As I sat down on the steps and strapped my rollerblades on, my nerves started humming. A few people brushed past me too close for comfort. Rex was safely locked away in our apartment, but was I safe?

To calm my nerves, I did the only thing I could think of. I climbed onto the scaffolding in front of the property and did pull-ups. I had never tried this with rollerblades before. I acted like it was just part of my routine. I was the rollerblade pull-up guy. Based on what I had witnessed so far, this seemed like the sort of thing that would pass as normal in New York. My fear subsided as I felt a safety bubble grow around me with every pull up. I had my business, and they had theirs. I kept dropping and pulling for as long as I could. Then I lowered myself back down to the sidewalk and quickly rollerbladed back to the bus stop. Within half an hour I was at the airport with Auntie Kelly.

She had been delayed twice at a layover and was exhausted. As we hopped back on the bus, her eyes were peeled wide. This bus ride at two a.m. idea kind of freaked her out. I was loving it. We were on a great adventure. Once we got off the bus and she got her skateboard under her, everything felt better. I made her a bowl of cereal and slept on the sectional next to Rex's sleeper sofa so she could have the bedroom.

Kelly was the reason I had rollerblades. When we hiked the Grand Canyon the month before, she told me I needed to get back to being me. She pointed out the stupid long hair I grew out for my ex, my ridiculous clothes, everything about me that wasn't me.

"You know what you should really do, bro?" she asked. "Go get some killer rollerblades and ride those around like you used to."

Kelly was right. I hated having long hair and I loved rollerblades. After the Grand Canyon, I went to the skate shop off Piedmont Park in Atlanta and got the best pair of skates they had. I started riding all over Atlanta several times a week. Once I went all the way down the Beltline and back from my condo, almost thirty miles. I went through one set of wheels and then another. For the next year or so, I took them on business trips and used them for exercise in the mornings and evenings.

The best urban hill in the South is the main drag in Columbia, South Carolina. It descends a steep hill through nine stop lights, and then shoots you out across a beautiful river bridge. If you time it right, you can hit all nine lights on green, and pass cars traveling at thirty miles per hour while you do it.

Since my car was dying, rollerblades became my backup plan of how to get the boys to school in the mornings. I timed out how long it would take me to push a big running stroller to Rex's school for kindergarten and then on to Rhett's preschool. I would keep Rhett with me as much as I could, but now I had a full-time sales rep working for me in Atlanta and I needed to use my home days to work with her. The whole loop to get both boys to school was just over twenty miles and took me nearly two hours with the stroller. I practiced it twice.

Luckily, I never had to use my rollerblades to get the boys to school. God kept my car alive right up until the right time.

Our last night in New York, Kelly and I found our element. We got out of Harlem and into the Algonquin Hotel on Times Square, and we went from being on a tight budget to balling out. We spent almost two hundred dollars on sushi where we watched five-year-old Rex eat his first dish of fish eggs. We had lobster rolls and saw Lady Liberty and went shopping at H&M. We weren't eating cereal and sleeping on the sofa anymore. We were living it up.

The Algonquin is a chic boutique hotel with a storied history you can see in pictures all over the lobby and up and down the hallways. Famous authors and politicians and journalists used to visit the hotel, especially the lounge called the Blue Room.

When we checked in, we found our room had a bed and a sofa sleeper, leaving us with a need for one more. I asked Rex to call the front desk to ask for a roll-away bed. He often called front desks to ask if they had seen his brother Rhett, who liked to disappear down hotel hallways. He knew just what to do.

He pushed the right button on the phone in the room and waited for reception to answer. "May I please have a roll-up bed?" Rex asked, nodding. "Yes, a roll-up bed."

He hung up and looked at me. "Dad, is a roll-up bed something I sleep on, or something I eat?"

I was high on endorphins from rollerblading six miles with him and our luggage on my back and started laughing uncontrollably. Auntie Kelly and Rex joined me, and we laughed until our legs weren't jelly anymore and we could move. I don't know if I even answered his question. We just laughed until we couldn't laugh anymore.

He didn't eat his bed. It arrived within minutes and was not made of candy.

The Algonquin also has a resident cat. We talked about it before we went to bed and Rex woke me up at five a.m. to go see the cat. He loves cats. We went down to the front desk a little after five, and there it was sitting on the reception desk waiting for him. The desk attendant motioned for me to lift him up on the counter to see the cat. Excited to oblige, and with only minimal help from me, Rex climbed onto the front desk to be with his new friend.

"This is the kid who wanted the roll-up bed?" asked the concierge with a twinkle in his eye, and then he asked Rex, "Well, how was your sleep, buddy?"

I couldn't believe this concierge had worked all night, from checking us in the day before to introducing Rex to the hotel cat this morning. I was impressed at how well he knew his little guest. The moment felt magical, and since we were in New York, I felt like we were spending a few moments with the gracious toy shop owner from *Home Alone 2*.

Rex was enthralled with the cat. I don't know my cats very well, but the Algonquin cat was a beautiful creature. She sat there for a minute and let Rex pet her, and then scampered away into her signature bed in the front window. Rex squealed with delight and tried to follow, but she was gone. Later that morning we saw her on display at her perch in that front window, next to some other hotel relics. She sat so still she could have been a stuffed animal. Auntie Kelly didn't believe it was a real cat. When we looked back, she was gone.

"See, Auntie Kelly!" Rex exclaimed excitedly. "We told you she was a real cat!"

That evening Kelly needed to work on a couple of school projects, so Rex and I explored the hotel while she used the business center. I used to have this thing for getting on rooftops. I've been on the roof of the Old North Church in Boston. That's the most notable for sure, but also fallen through the roof on a house in Puerto Penasco, Mexico. I've been on the roof of the haunted Brown Hotel in Denver and many other hotel rooftops.

I dare you to find another father-son duo who has snuck onto the roof of the Algonquin. We saw the ladder around the corner, on the top floor in the maintenance area, where there were several workers bustling around. Having already snuck into the dinosaur exhibit with me in Columbus, Rex knew to go into stealth mode. We crept closer until were only a few feet away from the workers; we hid just around a corner. If they came our direction we would be made, and the roof quest would be over. Luckily they bustled around a corner the opposite direction, and I quickly launched Rex up the ladder. The latch at the top was closed but opened with a push. We toppled out right onto the roof in the budding night lights around us. Like most places in New York City, it was filthy and noisy. We didn't stay long. Rex was hoping we would find the Algonquin cat up there, but a cat like her would not venture to a place like that.

Rex told Auntie Kelly we snuck onto the roof, and she didn't believe us. She claimed she still didn't think the cat was real either, that someone just moved it. Rex laughed as he tried to convince his auntie. I loved thinking of Rex through what might be the lens of his imagination. In his mind, he was in this crazy old building with edible beds and ghost cats where you sneak on roofs and break necks at every street corner riding on your bum on your auntie's skateboard. After such a challenging year going through divorce, the trip was everything I'd hoped it would be for him.

Rex drifted off into whatever dreams his magical imagination had in store as Kelly turned in her homework on time before midnight. She had done the same thing the night after we hiked the Grand Canyon. We were up late on the hotel computer finishing her homework in time to click "submit" at exactly 11:59.

But our last night in NYC, we weren't about to call it quits at midnight. We headed down to the Blue Room.

Kelly and I have stayed up late playing Scrabble since she learned how to spell. In a family of five kids, we are the night owls and the creatives. The wild ones. Of all our favorite evening activities, late night Scrabble held the crown. We played so much Scrabble I bought a travel Scrabble board with little pop-in tiles for camping. We took it with us to the Blue Room for an epic game of wordsmithing.

If you've never experienced the Blue Room, you are missing out. When the evening comes and they turn on the lights, it's lit almost entirely by blue, fluorescent lights. They turn everyone and everything a deep and glowing blue color. It's like entering the bioluminescent jungle world in the movie *Avatar* with Jake Sully for the first time. The booths and the bar preserve the cavalier American spirit that has remained in select parts of New York since the Revolution. The saxophones in the blues music matches the blue ambiance, and the acoustics are utterly immersive. There's a wall waterfall of bright blue water and beautiful, blue-based art on the walls. As blue goes, this is about as blue as it gets.

We brought out the Scrabble around one a.m. and played until three-thirty. At halftime, we needed a snack break and ordered from the one place nearby that delivered so late. We

ordered nachos, hummus, and vegetables, all the late-night crav-
ings. I had just enough cash on me to cover our total and tip.

We went home from New York on Thursday. As soon as I got
Rex to his mom, I was back on a plane flying to Utah to go on
a first date with a girl whose ex-husband I played high school
football with. I heard she had been mistreated, abandoned with
four kids and no child support. I felt like it was my duty to step
in and pick up where he so selfishly left off.

Chapter 4

The Same Damn Place

I WAS NOT HONORING THE TIMELINE ON MY VISION board by dating so soon. With all my trips back home to Utah, and the ease of using dating apps that didn't exist back when I got married, it was easy to thread dating into my schedule. But I was nowhere near ready for it. I should have been focused solely on helping my dad build a fence and visiting my mom for her birthday and rebuilding the other bridges I had burned during my marriage.

After a few weeks dating the girl my high school buddy had recently divorced, I started to notice myself entering a lot of the old habits that had gotten me into so much trouble in my marriage. Taking on her problems and doing so many things to make her happy, entertaining her talks of marriage after just a few dates. I lost myself. It was comical how predictable I was in a relationship. Give me someone to save and I was hooked. This was bad.

I had met Coraline once, the week I returned from my LDS mission. She was newly married to my high school friend, and they attended my homecoming speech together. I remembered thinking how pretty she was. Now she was divorced with five kids and no income, and he was not paying child support. My be-the-hero tendencies kicked in right away.

I flew to Utah and brought her a cake. After our date, I took her to dinner and had the server bring it out as dessert. She had no idea.

"Awww, that is so sweet!" she said. "I have been making cakes to pay the bills, but no one has given me one until now. Thank you. I love it!"

"You're welcome!" I said. "Everyone deserves a cake on their birthday. Especially after a busy afternoon like yours. I had no idea paddleboarding was going to be a stressor!"

"Well, it's not every day you go out with someone who has a coral eye. It's just so scary that I might lose it and then be eyeless. I mean I could wear the patch, but I'd rather not!"

"I get it," I said. "Kind of ironic that you have a piece of the ocean on you that stops you from going in the ocean. Again, I am sorry for the poor choice of activity!"

Coraline had explained how she had a rare and dangerous eye disorder as a child and had to have one eye removed. She had an expensive coral prosthetic in its place and had limited her activities in the open water her entire life to mitigate the risk of losing it.

I learned more about her and her dire financial situation. She desperately wanted to get married again. I lived in Georgia, and she was in Utah. There was no feasible way it could work. I asked my therapist about dating in the highly vulnerable state I was in, knowing full well that it was a bad idea. "Am I thinking clearly, in your opinion? Do you think dating so soon is in my best interests?" He answered yes and yes.

I needed better feedback.

My sister Kelly came to the rescue.

During a late-night Scrabble session, she gave me the feedback I needed.

"You fall hard, bro!" she said. "Better check yourself before you wreck yourself!"

We both broke into laughter. I saw scenes of Biggie Smalls "Respect" bumping across my mind . . . "better check myself, before I wreck myself . . . disrespect myself . . ."

Her tough love feedback could not have reached me at a better time. Her guidance was better than anything I ever got from any therapist. As our mom told us growing up: *old habits die hard.*

I still kept dating, but much more cautiously.

The next girl lived in Arizona but often came to Utah. I met her in Salt Lake City for a few days while on a work trip. Before long we were planning her trip to Atlanta. Her favorite author and speaker was putting on a seminar in a few weeks. I booked tickets.

In what ended up being a best-case scenario she ended up canceling. I found a friend to attend with me in her place. We strolled into the downtown Atlanta hotel conference room together, the only males in the audience. All the women in the room, the entourage of superfans there to see the host after months or years of following his Instagram, erupted in applause when he entered the room. His name was Stephan, pronounced the French way, "st-eh-fawn."

Stephan knew his room. He knew how much sauce to pour on which jokes, when to pause for laughter, when to ask for comments. I once attended a speech by Magic Johnson and was blown away at the way he captivated and interacted with a large audience. Stephan cast the same mystical power over these women in the room. I was awestruck at his control over his audience.

Not long into "The Truth about Love" seminar, during his introductory comments, Stephan told me exactly what I needed to hear.

"Then before long," he paced across the stage and spoke emphatically, "you're making excuses for the other person and compromising on things where you decided beforehand not to compromise. Then you're becoming a lesser person too, becoming dissatisfied, and now you're angry with yourself and with the other person. Before long you're stuck in the same damn place as you were in your last relationship, and nothing has changed. You're in hell!"

Making excuses for them: yes!

Compromising my non-negotiables: yes!

Becoming angry and resentful, while sheltering the other person from my feelings as they grow bigger and bigger: yes!

I was guilty on all counts. Stephan. He described me perfectly. Although I had heard and read similar things for years, it went in one ear and out the other. For whatever reason, probably because of my sister's help weeks earlier, this time it stuck. I motioned to my friend that I was ready to go, and we left early. I had what I needed.

No more dating during my healing time. I remembered a phone conversation with my mom years earlier.

"Matt, are your needs being met?" she asked. "I see you trying to meet Karen's needs and your kid's needs, but what about yours?"

"My needs?" I asked. "What do you mean?"

"Well," she answered, "you can't just do things for other people all the time, or eventually you're going to break. You need love and attention too."

At the time I fed my ego with my ability to do for others and hide myself, meeting my needs quickly and quietly when nobody could see. Sure enough, all the hot air from winning others' approval ran out of room in that thin and fragile psyche of mine, and I reached the place where my ego popped like a balloon. Mom was right.

I called the girl I was dating and told her I couldn't date her anymore. I did not tell her I came to that conclusion at her favorite person's seminar. During our phone call I crossed the Florida/Georgia line driving North from Jacksonville to Savannah. I decided to break my rule of only buying groceries while working and buy myself dinner.

I was not going to make the same mistakes over and over forever. I was listening to Stephan and doing right by me. I was going to stick to the vision board in my journal and take a few years off dating.

I peeled off at the Kingsland, Georgia freeway exit and found the best meal I could, considering it was after eight p.m. I routinely skipped meals or just didn't eat dinner. Not tonight. Tonight, I ate scallops and smiled at my newfound sense of hope in myself.

I recognized that most of life's meaning for me came from other people. My parents both grew up with people-pleasing complexes and I seemed to pick up on them. When I met Karen, I was studying journalism in college with plans to publish poetry and begin writing science fiction novels. Within a few months of meeting her I gave that up to earn a business degree and make money. I was just now writing again for the first time in nearly a decade.

I became obsessed with the full solar eclipse that was set to streak across the entire United States from Oregon to South

Carolina. I booked a work trip to Charleston so I could witness the full blackout for myself, hoping for a life changing experience. I decided to rollerblade onto the Arthur Ravenel Jr. Bridge, stretching across Charleston harbor, directly beneath the eye of the eclipse. When I reached the harbor twenty minutes before blackout, the pylons and ropes were out. The bridge was closed for the eclipse. I looked down at the hundreds if not thousands of boats that flecked the harbor beneath and beyond me.

I was determined to get the most epic view of the eclipse Charleston had to offer.

With no apparent security nearby, I slipped through the blockade. A security guard in a golf cart on the other side of the bridge hollered something at me, but he was enclosed on his sidewalk and would need to go across the bridge to get onto my sidewalk. I smiled and turned up the Metallica on my Bluetooth speaker to enjoy the view. I reached the center of the bridge minutes before totality and watched with my bare eyes as the midday sky became full of the Milky Way and the stars. I felt like an astronaut seeing the stars so clearly in the middle of the afternoon. I saw the golf cart cresting the bridge and coming down my sidewalk just before I raced down the opposite direction.

The eclipse was amazing, but the love story the eclipse led me to was transformative. While listening to a podcast about the eclipse, I learned about the love story of star-lover Carl Sagan and his colleague Ann Druyan.

The podcast featured Ann years after Carl's passing, as she discussed their unexpected romance. She talked about their journey into each other's hearts and out into the cosmos as they compiled their best description of life on earth onto a golden vinyl record sent to space on the satellite *Voyager.* I wept as I listened to their story. Even twenty years after Carl's passing, Ann spoke of their romance with fire and passion. She described his death in a hospital bed, as they gazed into each other's eyes and said goodbye. I longed for that kind of love. I had now made it through nearly one year of the timeline on my vision board. Two years to go. When I found love again, I wanted to find the Carl Sagan-Ann Druyan, astronomical-proportions universe-charting kind of love.

I read *Originals* by renowned business guru Adam Grant. It was the third important message that resonated in my soul. First Stephan's seminar, then Carl and Ann, and now this book. I realized that at this pivotal juncture in my life, I needed to challenge myself and try as many new things as I could. To rediscover myself and what made me tick. Everything was down the chute now, and it was a perfect time to start over without any limiting beliefs or expectations.

I started camping and staying at Airbnb's instead of hotels. Looking for interesting places to stay and unique people to meet. I booked flights for Scotland with my dad for the following January 2018. I visited Boston, Philadelphia, and Washington D.C. I read a book or two every week. I immersed myself in going, learning, and growing. I looked for myself everything I did. I looked everywhere.

I started with blogs, books, and blades. By late 2017, I was finally in the black, with extra cash flow on top of expenses and savings. I went to thrift stores and antique bookstores looking for old and rare books. I took my rollerblades everywhere. I found that I usually had at least three hours every day to read, write, and ride.

The more I tried doing things for myself, the worse I felt. I felt like I was walking weird, talking funny, my body felt strange.

I felt tired. As badly as I wanted to shed layers of pain and guilt and abuse, they held onto me. I was a failed parent and an adulterous husband. I wished I could quit my job and go hide in a hole. I hired people and tried to keep leading the pace in a company that had three hundred employees, yet I was falling behind. I couldn't tell a good hire from a crappy one. The problems I had with myself leaked out everywhere.

Something had to give. I needed an intervention.

While staying on a goat farm in Athens, Georgia, the Airbnb host invited me to a yoga class with her. I had been to a few yoga classes before but never hot yoga.

Bikram Yoga was about to expose my weakness and set me on the path to real healing.

I breathed as much cool fall air as I could while walking from my parked rental car to the Bikram yoga studio in downtown Athens to join the eight-p.m. class as a newbie. Yogis from the previous class looked like they had just gotten out of a sauna. I love saunas, so this didn't bother me. I signed a waiver without reading it, and one of the girls gave me a water bottle. I put it away in a locker. No water breaks for me.

The yogis in the room had their mats set up neatly in rows. All stood at attention, sort of reverent and quiet. These things resonated with me. I felt like I was back at football practice in high school. An instructor came into the room and barked loudly at us, clearly following a memorized script. She led us through an uncomfortable breathing exercise that made my shoulders feel like they didn't know how to move. The room, filled with maybe sixty students, had mirrors on four sides. The students moved together, breathed together, and I fell in with them. We moved through postures: holding, releasing, and breathing. I was dizzy because I didn't know how to breathe yet. I was so tightly wound and prehypertensive that it would take me many months to learn how to breathe. I felt like I might pass out. I kept a straight face and pretended to be fine.

I didn't like the way I looked in the mirrors. But I was determined to stare myself down and dig in. I had nothing positive to say to myself other than, "Don't break your posture. Hold strong and keep going." So that's what I did.

I loved being yelled at by the instructor. She was small and wiry and had the voice and the scars of someone who had learned who she was the hard way. I wanted her to yell at only me.

"Bend your knees! Up on your toes! Don't you dare stand up! Deeper! A little more, dig deeper! One more time!" She talked to me the way I talked to myself.

Far into the practice, we fell into what's called a camel pose. I didn't know how long we had been in it, or how much longer we would be, but I knew I would be there as long as anyone else. I felt like I was going to pass out, and I leaned into the feeling. If I passed out during a workout because I was too stubborn to quit, how badass would that be? I sunk down further into my knees, thrust my hips further forward, and bent my neck back, reaching for my heels like the voice commanded me to. Suddenly and unexpectedly, I began to sob. Out of nowhere I was crying loudly in the middle of a room full of silent yogis. I wanted to stop. I was not allowed to cry in public. I cried privately. My divorce taught me I needed to cry. I learned the therapeutic power of tears. But not in a room like this!

I felt ashamed and wanted to stop the pose and stop the blubbering, but immediately the instructor crouched right behind me, cradling my shoulders and my head.

"It's okay," she said. "Let it come. Sink into it."

And I did. Her touch and her words loosened me. Every pose we entered, she could see me holding myself tightly, flexing, keeping my body together, but when she told me to let go into the weeping camel, I felt like my hips fell out of their joints. Intense pain leaped out of them. I broke into tears. I held the pose while I cried. When she told us to come back up on our knees, I was still sobbing. She smiled at me as the class cooled down into the final poses. Tears blurring the sight of her, I smiled back.

"Where are you from?" She came up to me after class.

"Atlanta," I said.

"Have you ever done this before?" she asked.

"No," I said. I was glad I hadn't researched anything about the class ahead of time, and that I had let that experience happen organically.

"That was good for your first time. But you try way too hard. Looking around at everyone the whole time. Trying to be perfect. You have serious issues. Some of the worst I have seen. You need to learn how to relax. And you don't know how to breathe, either. You are a complete mess. And these puppies," she grabbed my hips, "these hold a *lot* of pain. You need to go see Cleve. Are you divorced?"

"Yes," I said. I was so surprised and overjoyed and embarrassed at the ninety minutes I had just spent feeling things I'd never felt before that I didn't know what to say. I decided to stop lifting weights, and to do this for as long as it took. It showed me the pain that needed attention, and I would visit it as often as I needed to.

"Hell yeah you are. You need help. I'm glad you came. Go find Cleve in Atlanta. Tell him Jo-Lynn sent you. Bye!" Jo-Lynn gave my shoulder a gentle squeeze as she scampered off to the next student who needed her.

"Thank you," I replied as she walked off.

Hell yeah, I would go find Cleve. I hoped he would cleave into me as well as she had that night.

Back at the goat farm, I sat naked in the hot tub late into the night and reflected on my maiden Bikram Yoga voyage. A lot of the yogis were clearly there as a rehab or recovery effort. I was perhaps more broken than anyone with a drug problem. My drug was ego. This yoga would be the thing to break me down. I had no ego in these poses that broke me open. I needed to learn to stop comparing, stop performing, and to start breathing. Feeling. Being. This was my path to enlightenment, like a priest going off to a monastery. I was determined and scared. Could I handle the pain that was down there? Could I face it? My hips and shoulders felt bad and weird when I tried to bend and move them in Bikram. I felt backward and awkward. The pain that welled up and poured out through tears and sobs was only the tip of the iceberg.

And the mirrors. The terrible, terrible mirrors. I hated looking at myself in those mirrors. I hated who I was. I judged myself so harshly. My abs looked flabby. When did I get so hairy? My jaws were tight. The dentist said I had been clenching my teeth. When did the lighthearted, playful me get old and stressed? Now that I took an honest look at myself, I saw so many problems. I felt so broken; I could finally admit it. These issues had brewed for years, but I didn't pay any attention, and neither did anyone else. Not closely enough to address these silent issues. I didn't look like me. Didn't sound like me. Didn't feel like me. I was someone else. I desperately wanted to heal and be me again.

The mirrors gave me an opportunity to face it. It was overwhelming. My eyes were dead. My feet looked flat and senseless.

Kneecaps were wobbly. Face was tense and stressed. I hated this person I had become after years of emotional abuse and self-neglect. In that hot, reflective yoga room, I knew I had to keep going until I loved myself again. This impossible yoga with these scathing mirrors was exactly what I needed. I wouldn't move forward with anything until I could look in one of those big floor-to-ceiling mirrors and see the man I wanted to see.

I had let myself cry in pain. I had let myself cry in sadness. I had learned to cry in my failure to stay married. But this cry that came in the yoga room was a different kind of cry. I didn't give it permission or see it coming. It came in the middle of a crowded room of sweaty bodies. That helped me start to gain self-awareness and acceptance. I was an iceberg and the me I had been seeing was only the tip. I saw there was so much more to surface.

I didn't know how many layers of ice I needed to get through, but I knew it would take years. I would go back into the yoga room and see myself in those mirrors for as long as it took.

Chapter 5

Bikram

IF YOU HAVEN'T BEEN THROUGH AN AUTHENTIC ninety-minute Bikram Yoga class for yourself, it might be hard to understand the level of commitment it takes to "stay in the room." Lots of yoga classes are full of students wearing Lululemon and whispering *namaste*. Bikram Yoga is not like that. Bikram Yoga is designed to break you. First you break a sweat: the room is heated to a hundred and five degrees. Then you can't breathe: humidity is set to ninety percent. Then you break focus: you look in the mirror and glare at yourself while you hold (and fail to hold) challenging postures for fifteen, thirty, sometimes even forty-five seconds. It's horrible.

Unless you are trying to heal. Then it's perfect.

It breaks you. And if you stick around to the end, it makes you high.

I Googled "Cleve Bikram Atlanta" and read how Cleve committed to yoga to heal from a drug addiction. Same as Jo-Lynn, who told me to find him. It made sense that recovering from a drug addiction was enough motivation to keep doing this brutal yoga practice year after year. I needed to commit to it too.

I was addicted to getting ego boosts from making people happy. I needed healing, and this was the first place I would find it.

When I went to my first class at *Still Hot Yoga* in Atlanta, the studio was buzzing about an ESPN documentary currently in production. The filmmakers had recently been to the studio and done some interviews for the documentary. I overheard conversations about the founder of Bikram yoga. After numerous lawsuits, he had recently become an international fugitive. His teachers across the globe were divided. There were essentially three groups. First, those who kept the name Bikram in their title and kept the yoga exactly how he taught it. They were fiercely dedicated and did not denounce their guru. There is an exact script to follow, exact amount of time per each of the twenty-six positions, etc. Second, there were those who removed the name Bikram from their practice but kept the yoga exactly the same. *Still Hot Yoga* fell in this bucket. Third, those who denounced Bikram completely after the scandal, and changed both their name and their practice. I read and watched what I could about Bikram Choudhury, the yogi fugitive who created these three types of followers. His narcissistic personality and revolutionary achievements reminded me of Kanye West.

I looked for Bikram studios everywhere I went. I looked for studios that fell into buckets one and two. I was not interested in bucket three. Everywhere I went, I had the same flaws. I was relentless in comparing my practice to the other students. Tying to *win*. I cared more about making the postures look good than building the fundamentals: balance, alignment, breath. I was still living off ego boosts. I went to extremes to create and preserve my image, to look strong, disciplined, and confident. I would stay in final *savasana* until everyone else had left, trying to look like I was never breaking focus, even though I was. I needed to be the best.

I observed these behaviors through those mirrors always watching me. I knew there was so much more than trying to be the best, and if I attended long enough, I would finally snap out of it. *Still Hot* didn't have early morning yoga every day, so I alternated between it and its sister studio *Be Hot* Yoga. One of the teachers at *Be Hot* had a podcast where she published a powerful episode about identity. As I listened, I cried. My entire life I had followed other people's directions and made other people happy. My religion, my marriage, my work. I had a very weak identity and lacked a sense of self. I hoped the mirrors in the yoga studios would show me who I was.

The high at the end of the Bikram class was often the only thing I could *feel* in my day. The rest of it I was a gray lump of senseless numb. But I tingled with delight after sweating out two gallons of water at the end of a Bikram class. Sometimes I cried, sometimes I peed a little, sometimes I blacked out for a few moments. No students ever had as much water around them as I did. It was part of how I tried to gain control during my divorce: excessive water drinking.

Nikki and I had done water drinking contests; the first one to a hundred ounces in a day won. By the time I stopped pretending to be in love with Nikki, I was routinely hitting a hundred before lunch. I moved it up to two hundred ounces per day and kept it there for over a year. I was so waterlogged I would cramp up, especially in the floor postures. I would sweat and sweat and sweat. In the postures where we went upside down, the internal part of my ears would fill with water, and I couldn't hear. Sometimes I got dizzy. But I wouldn't break the posture until the teacher said to.

Lying there in all that water at the end of class, I could hallucinate, go out of my body, become an insect, anything I wanted. I would hold an exhale for sixty or sometimes even ninety seconds. I called it oxygenating: removing stagnant air from my body.

I stopped lifting weights as often and started enjoying exercise for what it was, not just the results I sought. I let go of the need for comparing and performance and practiced receiving praise with grace. If I stripped myself down far enough, I would find myself.

I wouldn't move forward with any relationships. No dating until I was Matt again. Until then, I would keep digging and keep my pseudonym. Most of the people I met were through church, work, and yoga, where I introduced myself as Matthew. When people called me Matthew, they weren't talking to me but to this grief-stricken changeling. I felt like an alien. In yoga they refer to us as heavenly beings stuck in weird human bodies, and that resonated with me.

I kept up with Adam Grant's challenge in *Originals* to expose myself to new environments as much as possible. I read *Tools for Titans* by Tim Ferriss next and renewed my commitment to keep writing daily. By doing new things and digesting and incorporating them through writing, I would build back the awareness to bring me back to life.

Bikram Yoga helped me realize I had an extremely weak mind-body connection. To strengthen that connection, I dabbled in the appending disciplines of yoga. Extreme fasting, kundalini classes, ayurvedic dieting, guided meditation, sound therapy, whatever I could get my hands on. Eventually I decided to try a hundred-hour fast. The second day is the hardest. If you can make it to forty-eight hours, you can go as long as you want. But that doesn't mean you should. By day four, you feel like you are moving through water. You move, and then three seconds later, your body catches up. You start to feel your heartbeat in the tips of your fingers. I got past ninety hours twice, but not one hundred. I made a third attempt.

On day four of the fast I flew to Raleigh, NC to work with a guy I recently hired. He dropped me off at my hotel after our workday. I sat down for a moment, stood up too fast, and immediately blacked out. Feeling yourself pass out while standing is scary. I knew there was a desk behind me, a dresser to my right, and the footboard to my left, so I tried to relax and crumple down in place or slightly forward rather than sideways onto any of these obstacles. I surrendered to the blackness and went down. Everything quickly faded and I did not see where I landed.

I woke up after I don't know how long. I remained laying down, moving slowly while I looked over my body. Nothing broken or bleeding. I glanced at the clock. It was nearly midnight. I had hit hour ninety-six at about eight p.m. plus four hours: one hundred hours. I slowly trudged to the front desk for some snacks. When I got to the snack area, I felt like my body was still back trying to open the door to my room. It's hard to describe what four days with no food feels like. You move very slowly. I ate a Kind Bar with a side of Cheez-Its and felt more alive.

I made it past ninety-six hours, but never did I get to a hundred hours again.

Fasting made me more aware of what I put in my body. Now that I had killed the self-neglecting and people-pleasing cells in my body by starving them, I researched vegan. I watched the documentaries and believed the conspiracies about big businesses and hospitals and food. I bought a dehydrator and a Vitamix and made strange concoctions for my boys and me to eat. I stopped buying dairy, so we made a new nightly tradition of making our own ice cream in the Vitamix with frozen bananas and whatever add-ins they requested. There's chocolate banana, strawberry banana, and cookie dough. Bananas are versatile. But my favorite was plain banana with a pinch of cinnamon.

I kept wringing out my Bikram towel-mat and seeing black. I wondered whether I was getting cancer. The stress of my marriage must have created cancer cells, and I was probably seeing the evidence in these toxic black sweat particles.

I kept fasting but set the limit at seventy-two hours. I read that the most cancerous cells in your body are also the greediest; when you stop eating, they are the first to die. I was still worried I might have cancer from my destructive thought patterns. I operated on a calorie deficit almost every day to wipe out the cancer cells. My weight withered. Hundred-and-seventy, one-sixty, one-fifty, and even lower. I went all the way down to a hundred-and-forty pounds.

I kept fasting and going deeper and deeper to find myself. I believed that eventually I would. Six years in, three years out. By 2020, I would be myself again.

Chapter 6

Of Lochs and Livingstons

THE NAME LIVINGSTON COMES FROM A PLACE originally called "Levins Town" near Edinburgh in Scotland. I felt certain that while Dad and I were in Scotland, traipsing the halls of the castle our Scottish ancestors used to hide the Queen of Scots from her English enemies, I would find the missing parts of myself. Somewhere on the banks of the river where our predecessors fought for freedom with William Wallace, I would feel something.

The only time I felt anything was at the end of ninety minutes of yoga in a 105-degree room. I wanted to feel something else, somewhere else. And I really missed my dad. In the three years I set aside for healing and recovery, I made plans to visit and rebuild relationships with each of my family members. I flew home from Atlanta and visited my parents in Kanab probably a dozen times in 2017, but we usually just ended up doing "stuff" and making small talk. I wanted to have dedicated time away with each of them to spend time together. This was that time for me and my dad.

January was probably not the best month for the trip.

Early after our morning run, Dad and I met in the lobby of our little hostel in Balloch at the foot of Ben Lomond Mountain. The sun wasn't out yet, and the cold Scottish fog still pressed in on the little windows facing the rocky street.

"If we can catch the bus to Luss, we should be able to ride the ferry to Rowerdennan, and then we can hike Ben Lomond by lunchtime and be back down before it gets dark," said Dad.

He's a dreamer like me.

Google doesn't work nearly as quickly in the Scottish Highlands as it does in the States. Google showed all these services as "open" with hours and prices listed They were in fact closed. The bus doesn't go to Luss in the winter. The ferry had been closed since October. And Ben Lomond was utterly impassible even to mountaineers, covered in six feet or more of snow. I wanted us to go anyway. Hitchhike our way if we had to. I had to find myself. I might need a spot of frostbite and maybe a life-flight helicopter ride to get it done.

"I must be up there on the peaks of Ben Lomond!" I screamed inside. "That's where I'll find myself! We have to go!"

All I brought for the trip was a peacoat I bought on clearance sometime during my marriage and a backpack of books. Dad had the Green Bay Packers coat I got for him the previous year for his birthday. Ben Lomond would be a disaster. It was perfect.

Dreamer that he was, Dad felt this was within reach. We had been running like banshees in Scotland. Ten miles a morning both mornings in Edinburgh, bopping around the castles in Falkirk and Stirling. Our stamina was good, and he had gotten in amazing shape after being humbled by the Grand Canyon seven months earlier.

The hardest part of ascending Ben Lomond was getting the romanticized idea of a ferry ride out of Dad's mind. I knew the ferry was closed, and Google did too, but Dad still wanted this Luss-to-Rowerdennan ferry ride. He had a story about a ferry ride he told us kids many times. Some strange visitors to the ranch where he grew up arrived and asked his dad for directions. Grandpa Tom doesn't like anonymous visitors. With my six-year-old dad listening intently, Grandpa Tom gave the directions.

"If you're looking for that place, first you've got to cross over the dam that-a-way." Grandpa waved off to the west with some shooing hand motions. "Then you'll come to a fork in the road, turn right." More focused hand motions. "A few miles later you'll reach a ferry, get on the ferry to the other side of the lake."

Dad was so young he thought Grandpa Tom was talking about a pixie-type of fairy, so he stifled a laugh while Grandpa Tom finished.

"And once you've taken the ferry ride to the end," another fairy reference had my young dad's eyes gleaming with suspenseful joy, "you'll see the sign and know you've arrived."

Ferry rides were nostalgic for him. I had to convince him that we should do take the bus around the non-ferry side of the lake to Rowerdennan. Now was not the time to tell him Ben Lomond was closed and that to climb it right now would likely end in injury or death. First, I just had to get us into a spot where we weren't guaranteed to waste a day.

"Dad, the bus on the ferry side is closed," I reported, "but the bus on the same side as the mountain is open."

"Well, if we take that bus," he traced his finger just past where mine had stopped, "we can walk to the foot of the mountain if we need to!"

I left the rest unsaid.

We took the bus to the last stop, well shy of Ben Lomond. The roads were closed for ice and snow. However, there was another exciting hike where the bus left us. By the end of the hike, we ended up on a frozen mountaintop.

"Matt, we need to get out of here! This wind will blow us clean off the mountain. I am leaving *now*!" Dad yelled at me while I tried to hold a handstand in the whipping wind.

He turned on his heel and started his descent, leaving me alone on the bald meadow mountaintop. I looked out on Loch Lomond that seemed like miles below and imagined myself as a giant, skipping rocks across the choppy lake surface. I breathed the freezing air that stung my nose and eyes but filled my lungs with hope. I stood firmly on legs that I knew could handle the wind. Dad was overreacting. The wind wasn't *that* strong.

As I breathed and daydreamt, I felt peace I hadn't felt in a long time. I was just a kid on a hike with his dad. In the middle of winter in freezing temperatures without proper clothing or provisions. Still, I felt free.

I stood there and let myself, my Scottish self, my Scottish Livingston William Wallace self, feel free. I fought the effective-productive side of me that said, "Well, you're done here! Go join your dad, hike down, time to get out of here," and I just stood there.

I started to cry. I thought of what I had gone through to be in this moment feeling this freedom. I stayed married for seven years to try to make things work with Karen. I convinced her we needed a divorce. I spent tens of thousands of dollars I didn't have to get divorced so that I could spend time with my boys only to have them taken away from me. I fought for freedom and self-efficacy only to find that I didn't have a self anymore. For the year and a half since we broke up I struggled to find myself. Here I stood trying to have a self again. Trying to breathe. Trying to relax. Trying to smile.

Instead, just like when I tried yoga, I cried. Two difficult thoughts entered my mind while crying and looking out from the mountaintop. First, Karen wanted to move. This time to North Atlanta to be closer to "Ron Dad" and switch the boys' schools, again.

Second, my car really was going to die soon. The noises were getting weirder and worse. It would die any day.

I had a history of ignoring my problems until they became unbearable or solved themselves. Now I clearly saw that needed to change. I opened a note on my phone and wrote down a description of these two problems. I would face them head on.

Tears still streaming down my face, looking out on the fabled Loch Lomond beneath me, more problems surfaced in my mind.

I thought of how hard it was to be a father to divorced kids. I had never wanted that for Rex and Rhett. I wanted them to have the happiest home and the most enjoyable lives. Now they would have two homes for the rest of their childhood. Parent-time exchanges would interrupt their time with friends, movies, games. I was now what I had spent most of my life considering unimaginable.

And so, I said it, right there on the mountaintop.

"I am divorced, and that's okay."

As I said the words, more sobbing ensued. It felt good. I typed in my phone a ghost message to the boys, "Your mom and I are divorced, and that's okay." I would talk it through with them until we could be spectators of the situation and see it for what it was. We could get there. We were on our way.

I kept typing in my phone, "I feel guilty about divorcing her. Guilty about marrying her. Guilty about not having a two-parent home for my perfect boys. Guilty, guilty, guilty. It sucks."

The hundred-mile-an-hour winds wiped the tears from my eyes, and I felt better. I was learning to be honest with myself. I was learning to let freedom in. It was hard.

In the vicious winds beneath the Scottish sky, I felt my feet back under me, just a little. I felt like I had successfully called some parts of my soul back to myself. I scampered back around the icy-muddy trail to catch up with Dad, and we enjoyed the five-mile hike back down to the bus that took us to our little hostel where we rented one of just a few rooms.

We were both in the mood for something sweet, so we went to the French restaurant down the cobblestone street and ordered hot chocolates and a meringue. Dad is something of a savant when it comes to sweets.

"Dannng, they've got 'merannng' right here on the menu, don't see that every day, we better get one of those. Ever had a merinnnnngue, Matt?" asked Dad. He held the "angs" to emphasize his excitement.

"Yeah, of course, let's do it," I replied.

I was annoyed at the small talk, after all the deep introspection I had experienced on the mountain. With mounting resentment, unsure of how to transition to the deeper topics I yearned to discuss, I continued with him in the conversation.

He said, "It's kind of a French delicacy, really fancy, kind of like a soufflé but not quite. Ever had a soufflé, Matt?"

"Yeah, the pudding stuff, yep," I replied emptily.

"Meringue isn't the same as what's on the pie. Sometimes they get really big, and they get hard pretty fast, like an icicle. Wow, you've had a soufflé too? I haven't seen one of those in years." Dad spoke of the dessert like it was a rare and extinct buffalo.

He sat back with his eyes on me and slurped his hot chocolate. I could sense his awareness of my uneasiness.

I was still irritated because I was hiding from what I wanted to say. I didn't know how to admit to my dad I was starting from zero again and didn't have an identity. No, I hadn't tried those desserts. I didn't want to talk about desserts. I wanted to talk about family, failure, forgiveness.

I had never tried soufflé, never had meringue, never flown an airplane, never been to the Bahamas, never done a lot of the things my dad had done by the time he was my age. Instead, I married someone my dad warned me not to marry. I stayed married to her and now I was the worst thing of all: divorced. I was a quitter.

Facing that reality earlier on the mountain brought up impossible feelings. My ex-wife spent a lot of our relationship convincing me to turn against the people I loved, including my dad. He was my hero. I respected him for always finding a way to make it work with my mom. I felt like a disgrace. I wasn't measuring up. I felt stupid that Dad was right about her all along, from the afternoon two days before our wedding when he pleaded with me not to marry what he saw as a controlling narcissist whose father was even worse.

I had been yelling at him and putting him down for years at the behest of my ex-wife, and now I saw that he was so damn cool! And he *loved* me! I missed him so much, and now that we had a chance to bond and be real and honest, I was blowing it!

I saw myself closing off and shutting down. It was time to dig deeper and find a way into the conversation we both deserved.

The meringue came out as big as a basketball. After a few bites, I decided to break out of my shell and practice honesty.

"Dad, I've never had meringue or soufflé before, and I've picked up a bad habit over the years of lying and saying things just to look smart and control my image. The truth is I've had a big day, been going through a lot, and would love to talk to you about it."

"I bet you feel like a lot of the parts inside you died," Dad replied compassionately. "You left yourself behind for a long time. It takes a lot of time and attention to bring those parts back online. You have a lot of resolve to just keep going like you have, working and saving and all the time and making memories with the boys."

"Yeah," I choked on some tears, "It has been a lot."

"Well, I knew you had never had soufflé but wasn't sure about the meringue," Dad added, lightening the conversation. "Maybe we can get a soufflé before the end of the trip."

We sipped hot chocolate amid nibbles of meringue as we talked late into the night.

The next day, Dad and I sauntered into Falkirk just in time to find the perfect venue for Burns Night. They had exactly two seats left, so I bought them. Burns Night is like Scottish Thanksgiving, only with the addition of poetry and bagpipes. The most renowned piper in Scotland was playing that night, and the Vice President of the International Burns Society would be there to recite the poetry.

When we heard the bagpipes, we both cried like weaning wolf pups. The blaring sound of bagpipes resonated deep inside our Scottish souls. For hundreds of years, the sounds of bagpipes roused the Livingstons to action, commemorated their achievements, and brought them to the dinner table or banquet hall. We had never honored that part of our history together. We wept as we felt that stirring sound rouse memories inside that we didn't know were there.

We visited the castle our ancestors owned for a few decades during the Jacobite Rebellion and saw our name on the emblems of kings and princes. We walked tall around the castle grounds. Our ancestor, Alexander Livingston, became one of the highest Scottish lords simply by making allegiance with a former enemy. As soon as he declared his loyalty, the king gave him his eldest daughter as a wife and the Callendar House we were visiting as his estate. I'm pretty sure the King killed him later but still, the guy made history by jumping at an opportunity! I wanted to do that too!

We had seen the Livingston family crest in one of the stained-glass windows in Edinburgh Castle. We climbed to the top of the William Wallace monument and peered down on the elbow in the river where our forefathers had fought for their freedom. We read every story we could find and pressed locals for more details. We hiked and romanticized what it would have been like as a fifteenth century Livingston.

We ran every morning and ate big meals together at night. We copied accents we heard and re-enacted battle scenes and historical events, like when the Queen was smuggled into the Livingston castle in a suitcase to evade death threats of a rival. We decompressed over high tea and hot tub soaks at a gorgeous hotel near King's Cross before going our separate ways.

As I got on my train and Dad boarded his, my two big problems rolled across my mental landscape like graffiti on train cars.

"Your car is broken and will die any day!"

"Your ex-wife is going to move, and the boys will be in a terrible school!"

The week after Scotland, I went to Iceland. The week after Iceland, I went back to the Grand Canyon with my sister, Kelly. The week after that, I took new work clients to March Madness in Omaha, Nebraska. All the fun and meaningful experiences stopped me from worrying so much. I was excelling at work, too.

I signed three of the biggest deals of my career in one quarter. Things were looking up.

Learning to be myself was like being a toddler learning to walk again. The lights started coming back on. I made new agreements about who I was and what I could do with my life. I blogged every night, went to Bikram Yoga several times a week, and planned frequent adventures with my boys.

The Iceland trip was last minute. Over Christmas, my mom mentioned, "Matt, have you seen this WOW Air in Iceland? They will fly you to Europe for free."

I couldn't get it out of my head.

I Googled "WOW Air" and read an interview with their CEO that air travel would soon be free for passengers. In fact, airlines would soon pay the passengers to fly with them, rather than passengers buying tickets. Based on what I read, I needed to hurry and get this deal before they went out of business.

In between the trip to Scotland and to Havasu Falls with Kelly, I worked in Miami with my new friend Francesco.

Francesco came highly recommended. I asked him to pick me up at the airport and had him shadow me for the day. It was the funnest workday I ever had with a co-worker.

"The job is yours," I told him on the way to my hotel, "but I want you to say yes right now and start tomorrow. The other condition is I want you to teach me how to surf! What do you say?"

"You are speaking my language!" Francesco nodded in excitement. He grew up in Panama, where waves were life. "Sounds great bro! Let me confirm with my fiancée and I'll call you by the end of the night."

"Sounds like a plan, Capitan," I said with a Spanish flair, like cappy tan.

"Wait," he held up his hands, "how did you know that's my nickname?"

"When you know, you know," I replied cryptically. "I just felt it, you know?"

A few hours later he was officially hired. I wanted him with me the next day because I had an appointment with one of the largest furniture retailers in South Florida. We closed the deal and went surfing after. Whenever I flew down to Miami to work with him, he watched the wave charts and picked the best times for us to go, either before work or after.

One time working with Francesco, we finished Friday afternoon, and I had an appointment in Orlando on Monday. That left me with two completely free days. I remembered what my mom told me about cheap flights to Iceland. The flight left early that evening and returned Sunday. It was perfect. I used Amazon Prime Now to order a cheap windproof biking suit and some crampons to go over my shoes, booked a round-trip ticket to Reykjavik on WOW Air, and asked Francesco to rush me to Miami International Airport. I separated what I didn't need into a grocery bag and stuffed it in a rented airport locker.

I was on my way to Iceland.

Wow Air was a bare-bones experience, especially for a lengthy international flight. No Wi-Fi, no movies, not much to eat. But the round-trip halfway across the world and back was less than three hundred dollars.

I arrived around four a.m. and boarded a bus with a drop off near a glacier with a hot spring. I did a lot of Google Maps research before boarding the plane. I had become a Google Maps wizard during the impromptu hiring and selling I did in major cities across the South. Google Maps was my guide to life.

I was the only passenger on the bus. It was extremely cold.

"Huge storm blowing in," the driver hollered back at me. I nodded. We drove as wind and snow flurries swirled around us in the cold dark night.

"Huge storm blowing in," he said again the exact same way a few minutes later.

I was too busy watching the frosty snow flurries dance across the frozen icy road to give him anything but another nod. How was this itty-bitty track suit of mine going to keep me alive? I had heard the fire-breathing I learned in yoga could keep a body warm. I hoped it would work.

I did a quick asset assessment. What did I have? I memorized the bus routes from this glacier to the other mountain where I wanted to climb to my Airbnb. I had my little track suit and wore plastic crampons on my shoes. I had a backpack with lots of water and Larabars inside. I had an external phone charger, a headlamp with extra batteries, and a cheap pair of gloves. I would survive my twenty-four-hour adventure. Before lunch the next day, I would head back to the airport to return to Miami, get my stuff from the locker, rent a car and drive to Orlando. Sleep somewhere for a few hours and start work Monday morning. I would be fine.

It was pitch dark and frozen when I got off the bus at a small service station in a little town at the foot of the glacier where the hot spring bubbled up waiting for me. I walked past a steaming car full of what looked like sleeping hikers waiting for dawn. I would not wait, but would press on, headlamp lighting the way. I couldn't find the trail, but I knew the general direction of the hot spring. The ground was frozen solid.

I crested the glacier just as the sun did the same from the opposite direction, and we both smiled on the dark line of water that flowed down the center of the white landscape before me. It descended off to my left in a landmark Icelandic waterfall. It was a portrait in white. The sky was white, the clouds were white, the sun was white, the waterfall was mostly white, the only not-white thing anywhere to be seen was the line of water a mile in front of me cutting the glacial plane. I sped up my walk as I approached the little bridge near the pool I had seen on Google Maps.

The "geothermal" spring water was ice cold! I already had both my shoes off and fully immersed my feet before noticing. I was so cold that at first the water felt warm. It was not. This was ice cold water.

I could have booked time at the Blue Lagoon like everyone else, but I wanted to experience the real and raw Iceland, so I had decided to find my own glacial hot spring. Here I was after two hours of hiking and the water was cold! Not warm! I had been duped!

Am I going to get frostbite? I wondered. I felt a tinge of panic freckle my disappointment.

I had almost gotten frostbite as a kid on the ranch in Canada. My feet had nearly frozen after half a day out working with the cows in the dead of winter, but after growing up on John Wayne movies, I wasn't one to complain. I wanted to be a tough cowboy. It had taken hours of warm baths and blankets to finally warm my feet once inside the house.

The only towel I brought was from the Rams game I went to with Kyle a few months earlier. I used it to dry my wet and frozen feet and got back into my dress shoes with their rubber crampons. They fit over the shoes surprisingly well and seemed like a much-needed layer of insulation.

On my way back down the glacier, I passed that car of kids who were now headed for the same "swimming hole."

"Is this the way to the bridge?" they asked, still in the infancy of their hike.

"Yep," I replied without stopping. "It's there, all right."

The gas station at the bus stop was open when I got back. I bought Icelandic candy and waited for the bus. I rode it to my next adventure, a mountain overlooking the lake near Reykjavik. I would summit the mountain, return to the base, ride the bus to my Airbnb twenty minutes away in Reykjavik, sleep for a long time, and then head back to the airport. Good plan.

The mountain base parking lot was mostly empty, three cars total. Two of them were leaving.

"Dangerous time to hike, storm blowing in," one guy said in my direction as he motioned at the sky. I couldn't see anything.

While he broke down a metal walking stick and peeled off appropriate subzero temperature hiking layers, I did a quick stretch in my little track suit and began my ascent.

The snow on the trail was much deeper than it had been on the glacier. Small snow grouse danced and scampered on the barren ground around me. As I climbed, I turned back to bask in the views of the Norwegian Sea behind me. As cold as it was, the hike was gorgeous.

Then suddenly I couldn't see anything. I held my hand out in front of my face and could barely see it. I couldn't see the ground. Couldn't see my tracks to trace them back down the mountain. The storm had arrived. I had been so blinded by my intent to hike and so distracted by the beauty of Iceland that I didn't see the storm until it was too late.

I took a quick self-inventory and realized I was too tired. The waist-deep snow seemed like a good place to rest. That thought scared me. I had read and watched *Everest* and knew the risks of falling asleep in the snow. I determined to stay upright and moving to stave off the desire to sleep. I would stand and stay aware, and maybe I would get lucky. I figured I could stand there for a long time.

A faint light bobbed my way. As the light approached, a man appeared beneath it, running down the mountain dressed in what appeared to be a full astronaut suit with helmet and two ski poles for supports.

He yelled something that sounded like "Vike!" and kept running down the mountain.

I took that as an invitation to follow this astronaut Viking man down the mountain. I had to stay close to keep him in my sight. Clearly, he had done this before. When we reached the parking lot, he continued to the street and kept running while I waited at the adjacent bus stop for my ride. The bus soon arrived and took me into Reykjavik.

I walked from the closest bus stop to the little Airbnb I rented for the night. The room was in a small condo whose occupants were a young family with a cute bundled-up infant. The hosts did not speak English but quickly and quietly opened the door to show me to my room. I had Dominos delivered and ate the entire pizza. I slept for eleven hours. Then I took the bus back to the airport.

The airport is at least twenty miles from Reykjavik, a long and barren ride. The only notable stop along the way is the luxurious Blue Lagoon. I regretted trying to find my own hot spring instead of visiting the one right next to the airport that people come from all around the world to visit! *Wish I'd just spent the past twenty-four hours here,* I thought for a moment.

I remembered the Viking and the hiking.

No. I smiled as I looked out the bus window at the blustery, barren, chalky white landscape. *I would not trade that experience into the unknown backcountry of Iceland for the warmth of the lagoon. I believe I found a part of myself out there. To keep my calm when the snow rose up all around me, and to be there at the exact moment an astronaut Viking appeared to lead me down the mountain! The cold hot spring I could have done without, but the mountain miracle, that was amazing. For that, I am forever grateful.*

The storm grew so intense we barely made it to the airport. Large objects started rolling onto the road in the wind. Cars were pulled over to the side. The bus driver slowed down to twenty miles per hour. It seemed unlikely planes would take off. I checked my phone, no email yet from WOW Airline. Maybe I would get lucky.

We finally arrived at the airport. I checked in and got through security still hopeful but noticed the airport filling up with grounded travelers. An hour before my flight, the airport announced that all flights in and out were cancelled until the storm passed.

I still had received nothing from WOW. None of their workers were at the gate to give an update. I called the phone number, and no agents were available. They were going out of business sooner than anticipated. Not long after the announcement that flights were canceled, they announced that transportation in and out of the airport was cancelled, too.

I didn't have many options. I made the mistake of going back out through security, and now my ticket was void. I couldn't get back through to the restaurants and lounges.

I tried everywhere to get an answer about the next flight to the States. WOW only flew to Miami twice a week, so I wrote that off. Nobody was selling tickets at the airport, WOW's website was down, and now I was stuck in a small airport lobby with three hundred other people with no food and no warmth. The large sliding glass doors, the only thing separating us from a hundred-years blizzard, kept sliding open and closed for no apparent reason, blasting us with frozen air. I set up sleeping quarters beneath a table at Starbucks.

Before I fell asleep, I got an email from WOW that I had been rebooked on Friday's flight to Miami. Four and a half days from then. I dreamed of spending that time at the Blue Lagoon and again wished I'd just gone there.

I fell asleep between one and two a.m. and dreamt of a plumber banging on an exposed pipe. I wanted to tell him to stop, but he just kept on banging. When I blurrily woke up, it was a Starbucks worker doing a loud and repetitive task.

I kicked into gear and tried furiously to get a better ticket. The airport announced that an Iceland Air flight to somewhere on the East Coast was back on schedule for early that afternoon. A WOW flight to L.A. was back online, too. The WOW check-in counter was still closed. I tried to get a ticket on the Iceland Air flight, but it was overbooked. I tried the WOW website, but it was still down. I feared they had already gone out of business. I needed to get off that frozen island before they went belly-up! I called my brother and asked him to get me a WOW ticket to L.A. for that afternoon.

"Bro, can you get me the one-way to L.A. on WOW this afternoon and I'll Venmo you?" I begged him on the phone.

"Of course," he confirmed. "Cool that you get to go back to L.A.!" he replied, referring to our recent trip to the Rams game. A few minutes later I called him back.

"Did it work?" I asked.

"Yeah, bro, I got you, I'll email it to you. Good luck!"

I got the email and booked a second flight from L.A. to Orlando. Next, I booked a car to drive down at the end of the workday and get my stuff. I would lose a day, but it could have been worse.

It was early morning in Orlando. I texted my sales rep there and let him know I needed a personal day and would work with him tomorrow.

The new plan went off without a hitch. I emailed WOW detailed expenses for reimbursement. They went out of business before granting my request. What should have been a two-day, three-hundred-dollar trip became a four-day frozen nightmare that cost me almost a thousand dollars. Two extra days of food, an extra transcontinental flight, then another flight to get to Florida, plus a rental car. Still, I had pulled it off without any serious interruption to my work and home life.

After a few days in Orlando, I flew to Las Vegas for my Havasu waterfall hike with Kelly. I had nothing but a small backpack, with no winter clothes. I wore tight-fitting jean shorts and a bulging muscle shirt as usual.

"Ha ha, I hope you brought more than that, bro!." my sister said, laughing. We had a twelve-mile night hike a few hours ahead of us. "It's gonna be cold tonight!"

"Cold!" I scoffed. "I came here to get warm. I thought I was getting out of the cold! I went to Scotland and Iceland for that. It can't be that bad, right?"

"I guess we'll see," she replied.

That night, we parked around midnight and got out of Kelly's car to begin the canyon descent to Havasu Falls. It was close to freezing and had started to rain.

I stood in my skin-tight jean shorts and t-shirt while she laughed.

"City boy," she laughed, "in your twelve-year-old shorts and your twelve-year-old t-shirt! Ha ha!"

I laughed with her. Her criticisms were always endearing to me.

"Do you have an extra hoodie?" I shivered out the words through my laughter.

She tossed me a hoodie from her trunk.

About sixteen hours later we had enjoyed the hike and the waterfalls, and a short nap in our hammocks. A frozen wet kiss on my forehead woke me. It was a snowflake.

"Snow!" I exclaimed, nearly falling out of my hammock. "Are you kidding me?"

"That's why you always come prepared, bro." Kelly handed me a hand-warmer from her CamelBak. "Look at that sky! This is only gonna get worse."

Just a few hours after reaching our destination, we began the twelve-mile hike back up and out of the canyon. Darkness fell and we got disoriented on the wide canyon floor. We were approaching forty-eight hours with only one hour of sleep. Neither of us had done this hike before. There's a point where you turn to reach the parking lot, and we thought we might have passed it. The snow was still coming down and it was at or below freezing. I was still wearing shorts.

"Coyote!" Kelly yelled, startled. A hundred yards in front of us, in the beam of the flashlight, I saw him too.

"Here to guide us home," I replied. We followed him. He disappeared just as we reached the turn to the parking lot.

We drove through a full-blown snowstorm, barely able to see the road. We stayed the night in Kingman. We slept in until right before the hotel breakfast closed, ate, then Kelly took me back to the Las Vegas airport.

In Atlanta, feeling high on life after all my adventures, I called Karen from the metro on the ride home.

"I don't think you should move again," I told her. "The boys have been through a lot, and they are in the best elementary school. Rex just finished kindergarten and has friends in the area, and next year Rhett will do the same. We need to keep them here. You can't move like this."

My heart fluttered like a hummingbird the entire time I talked. I had never been this direct with her before. I braced for the yelling that would come back at me, the many things I had done wrong, her list of complaints.

Instead, she said, "Okay." I was finding my voice, and we were creating some stability.

Outside my condo building, I went to grab something out of my car, but it was gone.

I specifically remembered parking, because it had been raining when I left. The car was gone. I had spent a year and a half in constant anxiety waiting for it to die. Gotten two tickets for driving with an expired registration. Now it vanishes. It was time to move on. I thought back in gratitude for the tough year that car got me through.

I emailed my property manager who responded that she had a notice from the city. Since I had parked on a city curb, with an expired registration, the car had been impounded. It would cost more to get it back than it was worth. Yes, it was time to move on.

I quickly found a 2002 Toyota 4Runner for sale on Facebook Marketplace. It was perfect for me and the boys to get around Atlanta and go on adventures across the South. We celebrated by flying Auntie Kelly out the week after I bought it. We all drove to the beach together. It was perfect for us. I was finally driving without the fear and anxiety of wondering at what moment my car would go kaput. More freedom crept in. It hadn't even been two years yet of the three I had allocated for my recovery. I felt like I was on track.

A big part of that was daring to say no. After thirty years of people-pleasing, I had learned to say no. I refused to pay unfair attorney fees, and that gave me the funds to buy a car. Standing up for myself was the best thing I could do for myself.

Everything changed after that. At work, when I had to make big decisions, I moved at lightning speed. I signed another huge deal, my biggest ever, for the third time in 2018. I hired the two best Area Sales Managers in the now half-billion-dollar company we were building. The year wasn't half over yet, and I had already hit my targets. I still felt empty and angry inside, but it didn't slow me down like before. I was taking control and rebuilding my life.

Chapter 7

I Am Ruth

I THOUGHT ABOUT WRITING A BOOK BUT DIDN'T know how. I journaled every day, blogged every night, and prepared myself to write books. I had an idea for a book series, but I needed a few years of practice. My brain had a harder time putting words together. I had mental blocks and destructive thoughts after getting divorced.

I tried writing a book about the divorce, but it was too painful. I had a lot of ground to make up before I could forgive Karen. Journaling helped.

The summer flew by. Rhett learned how to swim. Auntie Kelly and I got helmets and flashlights and took the boys through the pancake squeeze in Pettijohn's Cave. I purchased a fitted suit for myself.

I made another great hire in my home base of Atlanta. He quickly became a friend just like Francesco had. We would meet up early and get fresh squeezed juice before our workday. I could not believe how cool the people were who were coming into my work circle.

The trip Dad and I took got us right back into the swing of each other's lives. He forgave me for cutting him out of my life for so long. I needed the same sort of experience with my mom. She had her own pains because of a difficult relationship with her mom and my middle sister.

Francesco and his wife announced their wedding for the following February in Panama. I RSVP'd and decided to bring my mom along with me. It was only a few months until Mom's birthday, which would be a great time to extend the invite. I reached out to my brothers and sisters about surprising her with a birthday party. I was the only one living outside Utah. Everyone quickly confirmed.

Mom and I were bound for the tropics! I knew she would accept the invite.

I took my new Atlanta hire with me to a convention in New York. After the trip with Rex and Auntie Kelly, New York had become my favorite place to rollerblade. We stayed at the Essex House across the street from Central Park. On our first morning there I woke up early and skated four loops of Central Park. Each loop is something like six miles.

Later that day, during another rollerblade break, I pushed it too far.

For a year or so I had wanted to rollerblade the Brooklyn Bridge. I put on my speedo and went in the middle of the day. I whipped my phone out on the way down and Snapchatted myself going forty miles per hour (the same speed as cars; the speed limit there is forty-five. Snapchat has this cool feature where it shows your speed) amid crazed looks from drivers and lots of honking.

Then there was a break in the cement. I was going too fast. I had never hit forty before. I didn't care. The adrenaline was there, and I was going as hard as I could, let the consequences come.

Cars were all around boxing me in. I did my best to gently bunny hop the crack. I closed my eyes and hoped I would hold it together. Somehow, I didn't crash. I rode out the bridge and finally came to a stop at the outdoor sports complex on the Brooklyn side. I rolled to a stop and sat down, removed my rollerblades, put on some shoes from my drawstring backpack, and jumped in the next pickup game.

I met my new hire Charles and my colleague and close friend Michele at the convention dinner that evening. Michele and I had worked through the growing pains of building a company together.

I showed them the Snapchat video. Michele interrupted my commentary.

"I'm sorry, but that is crazy," she said. "I know you're Superman, but you need to stop. Do you realize you should probably be dead right now?"

I was stunned. Normally, my reckless feats received praise. Not criticism.

"You have kids! Do you realize how irresponsible that is? Riding your rollerblades through busy traffic at high speeds, in New York City, of all places? On the Brooklyn freaking Bridge? You need to stop, Matt. That is so, so dangerous. Promise me you will never do that again."

Her fiery eyes met mine. Her voice cracked with emotion. I could tell she cared about me. It meant a lot.

As I responded, I stepped out of myself for a moment and considered the gravity of her words. Had I tried so hard to feel something again that I kept putting my life in danger? I thought about when I passed out fasting. I had numbed myself to reduce the sting of being a failed spouse, and therefore a failed parent. Now, I was pushing the limits way too far.

Us Tauruses are very particular about our image. I felt ashamed of being a divorced father. I would accept it eventually, but meanwhile I numbed myself to make it bearable. I knew Michele was right.

Even though I swore never to fast ninety-six hours again, I still routinely completed two and three-day fasts. I still did Bikram Yoga daily and often completed multiple ninety-minute sessions. Extreme rollerblading. I learned about the chakras and full-moon sound baths and Reiki and tried all sorts of ritualistic experiments. Tauruses go hard, too; we tend to take things to the extreme. No half measures.

I was cleansing myself from years of abuse while trying to feel again. And it was working. I felt better than I could ever remember, but I needed to calm down and trust the process. Quit trying to speed it up rather than letting healing take its course.

I love Michele for what she taught me that day. I hung up the rollerblades and let them become just a hobby. No more traffic violations or speed records. She loved me, and she was right.

I had blogged every night for months, had written dozens and dozens of posts, and I decided in September to start on a book. As a young journalist in high school, I had aspired to start a publishing company for real people writing real stories. Memoirs, novels, fantasy, all of it. I had long since given up on those dreams, but I was back to being me now and the writing slowly came back into focus.

Writing felt awkward and ugly, like I was trying to throw a football with my left hand or spell my name with a pen held in my toes. Yet, I made progress.

I taught a lot of Sunday lessons at church, and in the summer of 2018, I came across the Book of Ruth in the Bible. It's one of my favorites. The redemptive side of it reminded me of my story and how I hoped to end up with a woman I liked and who liked me too. I had turned off a lot of my feelings the previous year, feelings of failure and regret, and writing required me to turn them back on. It was painful and messy, and I felt out of control again. There were so many things about my failed marriage I had yet to confront. Betraying my friends and family. Telling myself I didn't matter. Lying to myself to make my marriage bearable.

When I read Ruth, I identified with her. She sought a relationship based on her faith. She trusted her beliefs and worked through incredible adversity waiting for things to work out. I *was* Ruth. I wrote about my divorce in a stream of consciousness style as if I were the wife. Since I had taken on the traditionally feminine roles in my household—cooking, cleaning, bathing and dressing and feeding the kids—it came naturally to write from the perspective of a woman.

I wrote through the lens of female eyes and what I/she felt and thought and did before her marriage ended. I wrote an entire book about the thoughts and feelings that took place in that one day when the divorce started.

I would time-block a few hours once or twice a week to write. It took a toll on me. I would break down crying, thinking back on the weeks I didn't get to see Rex and Rhett. I would start trembling when I thought about my mom, whom I had all but completely removed from my previous married life, driving back across the country with us in a futile attempt to restore our lives to normal. When I thought about Karen, and her verbal abuse, I screamed and cried as I typed away on the MacBook. I pounded the floor and sobbed into the hardwood and typed on the MacBook. I puked and pooped and convulsed and typed away on the MacBook. I wouldn't stop until it was all out of me. There was so much poison left behind from my toxic relationship with Karen and my self-loathing for being a divorced dad.

I had exercised so much the past two years that I was always hungry. Every time I sat down to write, I needed to eat. I couldn't afford to support extra muscle mass and write a book at the same time. I had just run a triathlon and won my age group. I spent time at the gym when not doing Bikram. There weren't enough hours. I stopped lifting weights. Yoga only. That way I wouldn't need to eat. I already knew how to fast four days straight and could survive on soup and salad. I would make the sacrifice and write the book.

Between September 2018 and February 2019 while I let my feelings flow into that hundred-page memoir, I lost even more weight. I'd already dropped from one hundred eighty pounds to one hundred forty. I'd crack the one thirties by the time Mom and I got to Bocas Town in Panama.

My work trips to Miami when I would surf with Francesco became a source of solace. Francesco taught me how to relax. Normally, I would go straight from working to writing to cleaning or something else, always busy. He helped me see that I was too tightly wound, feeding into my own anxiety, and that I needed to relax. Every workday in Miami included a trip to the beach either before or after work, either to surf or to wind down. I allowed myself more down time.

Francesco was gearing up for his wedding the next February in Bocas del Toro, Panama, close to where he grew up. He showed me pictures of the venue and the breathtaking villas we would stay in as part of the wedding party. He told me about the waves and the food. It sounded phenomenal.

During the trip, Mom could help me edit the book as we used our time together to talk and to heal. I had tried opening up to her a few times since the divorce, but there was too much unresolved conflict between us. We both held back a lot of our pain and tried to hide it. We didn't want to inconvenience each other.

That needed to come to an end. I couldn't believe, looking back, that Brian Adams convinced me to stop talking to my mother during my marriage. I felt guilty and needed time and space to truly express my regret to my mom.

Getting ready for my trip to Utah to surprise Mom for her birthday, I looked through my baby book at the pictures of her reading to me and playing and smiling at me. I loved the way she looked at me with such adoration and love in the pictures. Now she avoided looking at me; she thought I didn't love her anymore.

That pain was three-fold. First, I was undeserving of her love because I rejected it. I felt awful for abandoning my mom. I had married someone who verbally abused her and wouldn't let her see her grandbabies.

Second, I hated that Rex and Rhett would never have pictures of a mother looking and laughing and reading with them with love and adoration.

Third, deep down I still felt bad for abandoning Karen in the divorce. She had been mistreated her entire life and suffered from mental illnesses that were not her fault. How could I have left her like that? Why couldn't I have kept bearing that cross and stick it out with her, miserable though I was?

Those walls came up when I tried talking to Mom again. I could tell she had some of her own. Neither one of us knew how to break through them. Not yet. If we could spend ten days together, in love and honesty and serenity, we could get through them.

We surprised Mom as she and Dad were seated at one of their favorite restaurants. Mom screamed with delight and hugged us. We had a cake, and we had written a series of childhood memories in a poem Dad read her. Her favorite thing in the world was having her kids together.

We got back to Kanab that evening. Mom sat at the table opening some of the gifts we gave her. I decided to tell her my big news.

"Mom, my friend from work is getting married in Panama next February, and I want you to come with me!" I practically shrieked.

Mom's eyes grew big. She loved the beach but did not often go.

"We can stay in a jungle bungalow on the beach and snorkel and play with monkeys and go to a cacao farm! It looks like the most amazing place, and I have it all planned out!" I continued. "So, will you come?"

Mom sat silently, digesting the invitation. I pulled up the Airbnb listing of the bungalow we would stay in for the first week, and the resort digs for the weekend of the wedding. I had already booked everything.

Mom thumbed through the pictures but still said nothing. She loves the ocean. It's one of her favorite things. When she studied at BYU, she took a semester at the Hawaii campus on Oahu so she could be near the ocean. Our two best vacations while growing up in Kanab were both trips to the beach.

She looked up at me after seeing the pictures, still speechless, then back at the pictures again. Finally, she looked up at me and pointed down at the pictures on my phone. "We get to stay there? Really?"

Her question was so tender I wanted to cry and give her a hug. There was still so much distance between us. This interaction was awkward for both of us. We needed this trip.

"Yep!" I smiled.

"Well, of course I'm going!" Mom jumped up and danced around the house. "I get to go to Panama! I get to go to Panama!" She switched off between dancing around and sitting in the red recliner Googling "Bocas del Toro" on her laptop.

After I returned to Atlanta, I started calling Mom after my writing sessions to read her what I wrote.

In writing, I found honesty. In that honesty, I found forgiveness. I forgave myself for mistreating my loved ones. I forgave Karen for being abusive. The toxicity kept seeping out of me. The tightness in my jaw started to loosen, the anxiety in my chest started to fade. Days got brighter. I let myself believe I had value again.

I woke up early at sunrise and read my scriptures. I was reading the Sermon on the Mount almost every day, my favorite passage of scripture. That was a big part of the reason I was able to forgive Karen and take accountability for our failed marriage. Jesus says love and forgive, and after I heard it about a hundred and fifty times, it finally happened. I wasn't thinking about making it happen, or even aware it needed to. But that morning as I was read, I felt love and forgiveness enter my heart. I didn't need to blame her to protect my own ego anymore. I was at fault for a lot of what happened. I stared out my high-rise window as the sun rose over Buckhead Atlanta and felt liberated from the self-judgment I had carried for the past two years since we separated.

Chapter 8

A Year in the Mirror

HELLO, THIS IS THE DISNEY EMERGENCY RELOCA-
tion team. May I speak with Matthew Livingston?" asked
the Disney representative.

"Yes, this is he," I replied as the clouds above us gathered for
another stormy night.

"We haven't heard from you yet, and you are the last family
still at the Wilderness Camp," she said with concern in her voice.
"Hurricane-speed winds came through last night, and they are
expected to worsen tonight. We are closing the camp and evacu-
ating you to a hotel for the rest of your stay. How many guests
are in your party? Does the All-Star Music Resort work for you?"

"My sisters arrive tonight," I replied, thinking how ever-
adventurous Auntie Kelly would be bummed not to camp in a
tropical storm. "Could we have two double rooms?"

"Oh, yes, absolutely. Just head on over as soon as you can.
Your rooms are ready."

"Thank you," I replied. "We brought mostly food to prepare
on a camp stove. Since we are switching to living indoors, would
you be able to add a food credit to the rooms?"

"Oh, sure, Mr. Livingston," she replied right away, "The rooms do come with breakfast with Mickey for free. You just need to schedule a time in the Disney app. I'll also add a hundred dollars food and beverage credit per room per night and upgrade your wristbands to Fast Pass wristbands for when you enjoy the resort. Anything else?"

The boys were sound asleep. After midnight I departed on the Disney bus to pick up my sisters from the airport.

"So, I have some good news and some bad news," I told them after hugs. "What do you want first?"

We had the large bus with comfortable seats and whimsical Disney music all to ourselves on the empty freeway.

"Bad news first!" Auntie Kelly said. "Always the bad news first so we get to end on a high note."

"That's fair," I agreed. "Okay, so you know how these falls in the South can be. There are currently some mild hurricane warnings, so we got evacuated from the campground."

"What!" Auntie Kelly lamented. "Why does this always happen? First, it's the lobster trip two years ago, then last year our shrimp and grits festival got hurricaned out, and now I don't get to camp at the most magical campground in the world with my neph-pups? You better have some killer good news bro!"

Lindsay added, laughing, "If there are so many hurricanes in the Fall why do you guys keep planning trips at this time of year?"

Kelly and I looked at each other, stunned at our own foolishness. We burst into laughter and got ready for the good news.

"The good news is, you guys get your own room, we are across the hall, they upgraded us to FastPass and we get $200 of free food at the park!"

"Yusss!" Kelly said. "That's what I'm talking about! I'm still pissed we won't get to go gator hunting at the campground, but that rocks bro. Nice work!"

"To be honest," added Lindsay, "I can live without the camping. Can't wait to see Harry Potter world tomorrow! I think it will be more fun after a good sleep in a real bed."

I had full Harry Potter gear for Rex and Rhett to wear the next day. I loved the anonymity of dressing up like someone else on Halloween. More than that, I took full advantage of the permission to wear little to no clothing one night of the year. I had been Adam in the Garden of Eden, Aladdin, Tarzan, a native warrior—these are my kinds of costumes. Lingering behind that joy of being someone else for the evening was a true lack of identity and craving to be someone else permanently.

Kelly had been justified in her lamenting about our failed Fall vacation plans. The prior September we had tickets to a beach festival in Jekyll Island that got canceled because of hurricane warnings. We still went and had an adventurous day exploring the famed driftwood beaches of the island. Our first evening we put the boys in a tent between our hammocks like usual.

When I woke up and washed my face in the campground bathroom the next morning, I looked up at the mirror and saw a picture frame instead. The guy in the picture looked kind of like me but had dozens of bright red spots all over his face. *Why did they put a picture here instead of a mirror?* I wondered. I looked over the sink next to me for a moment, and quickly realized it was a mirror. But that meant . . . Oh no! What happened to my face?

I splashed water in my face and rubbed my cheeks and forehead furiously with my hands, hoping to splash myself out of this nightmare. I moved my hands to the countertop to ground myself. I took a deep breath and looked up. My face was the same. I stared closer and breathed a sigh of relief as I realized I had been attacked by gnats in the night, or as they call them in the South, "no-see-ems." They didn't itch too badly. I would be fine.

"Bro, what happened to you?" asked Kelly as I walked back to our site.

"Bug bites," I mumbled grumpily. "I didn't even recognize myself!"

"Those are gnarly, bro! Do they hurt?"

"Not too bad," I replied, laughing it off as my sister chuckled. "Mostly just embarrassing. Have you checked the weather report? It's looking cloudy."

"Yea, dude," she replied, "we gotta go. It's already up to a category 2, and it's passing the Florida/Georgia border right now. Let's move."

I looked at her hurricane map. It was moving North at around fifty mph, and it was only about fifty miles away from us. She was right; it was time to go.

"Okay, boys," I called out, "we will eat breakfast in the car. There's a big storm coming and we gotta go!"

By the time we pulled onto the freeway we could see the storm behind us about twenty miles away. We were cutting it close. Google seemed to think the storm was going slower than freeway speeds, but hurricanes are unpredictable. I was glad we had a different car than the Corolla I had limped along with for a year and a half as the engine started to give out.

I floored the 4Runner, and we raced north to the interchange that would take us west to Atlanta. I glanced nervously in the rearview mirror as we played games and told stories, watching videos on Kelly's phone of our adventures from the last day.

"Um, daddy?" Rex called out. "Is that the storm?"

I looked out his window at the darkened sky, the thick rain-clouds, the lightning, and strong winds. The storm was as far north as we were. It had caught us.

We were only a few miles from the Savannah interchange that would take us west and out of the path of the hurricane.

"Rex, you found it," I said as calmly as I could. "That's why we left the beach, and we are 'bout to turn the other direction so we can escape it."

"You better hurry, Daddy!" said Rex. "It looks like it might lift us away!"

He was right. I had seen footage earlier that year of a frisbee wedged eight inches into the top of a palm tree during a hurricane. These storms were no joke.

We turned west, and the storm faded into the skyline behind us. We hadn't eaten much breakfast and had a cooler full of food to cook on my camp grill. We pulled off the freeway and found an elementary school playground for brunch. The boys scampered to the playground while Kelly helped me prepare lunch. I hadn't used the camp stove in a while, and accidentally let the propane flow for a minute or two before lighting it.

Whooooosh!

When I finally lit the stove, the excess invisible and nearly odorless propane had flowed out across the picnic table and onto my arms. It erupted in a volcanic blast of fire as I leapt backwards in surprise. Auntie Kelly was crouched over the cooler, looking another direction. She quickly jumped to her feet.

"Whoa!" she exclaimed. "What the heck was that?"

The fire died as quickly as it had leapt to life. Kelly felt the heat and heard the noise but didn't see the flames. I hit my face and arms with my hands to make sure I wasn't on fire. I smelled that odor from calf brandings on the ranch. My arm hair was completely gone.

"I, uh, I . . ." My voice trailed off.

"Sounds like you almost blew up the camp stove!"

"Um," I replied, too embarrassed to admit my folly.

"Bro!" she lifted her hand to her face to cover a laugh. "Your eyebrows are gone!"

"What!" I exclaimed, reaching toward my eyes, hoping she was joking. I felt short and curly hairs that had been badly singed by the camp stove volcano.

We erupted in laughter and my jitters calmed. I had gotten off easy. It could have been much worse.

"Not every day you survive a hurricane and an explosion," I concluded. "Let's eat!"

November marked the anniversary of the day I first walked into a Bikram Yoga studio. I had done over 300 sessions since that day. I arrived early and stayed late to stare at myself in those mirrors, waiting for something to happen. I regularly visited the major cities in the Southeast. I found Bikram studios in Tampa, Orlando, Miami, Jacksonville, Charlotte, Greenville, and Columbia. They all had six a.m. classes making it easy to fit in a workday. I became a regular student of a Bikram practice in each city. I got to know the teachers, who were often the owners.

Early on the day of my yoga-versary, I arrived early at the Bikram studio in Jacksonville Beach, Florida. Rob was one of the most memorable yoga teachers I ever had. He taught Bikram in a little house converted into a yoga studio on Beach Boulevard. The beach house didn't have central heating, so he raised the room to the required hundred and five degrees and forty percent humidity using a large commercial grade blow torch. I found it interesting that Rob didn't have us sign a waiver walking near that torch.

"Welcome back," said Rob as he greeted me. "Don't get too close to the torch. I set it a little higher today from the cold front."

"Yeah, that puppy is scorching today, love it. We were in Disney's campground a couple weeks ago for the storm until they moved us into a hotel. I have never felt it this cold out here before."

"Wow, that's crazy," he replied in his professional monotone voice. "Yeah, I have lived here twenty years, and this is one of the coldest Novembers I can remember. You showering today?"

"Yes sir, as long as that's still okay," I replied. The house had an enclosed shower outside on the deck. Rob let me use it to get ready for work instead of having to go back to my hotel.

In the 300-plus Bikram Yoga sessions I had completed in the past year, I had never yet taken a rest during a class. Never taken a break. Never had a sip of water. I considered those concessions to be signs of weakness. I was trying to be perfect in my practice so I could find myself. But that day, November 14, 2018, I took a little joy in my practice. I tried to find myself in a different way. When my heart felt like it might explode, I knelt on my mat and did some deep breathing, instead of slaving through it like normal.

Rob walked by and placed his hand on my shoulder. "Good," he said.

It didn't feel weak, or inferior, or less than. It felt good. I looked in the mirror and saw for the first time what looked like a little smile on my face.

One of the teachers who rotated through the Bikram studio in Atlanta had her own podcast. She taught only on Fridays.

I loved her classes because she gave lectures while teaching, and she was one of the few who could see right through my perfectionist tendencies to the broken soul inside. She would walk up to me in the middle of class and grab me by the ear or the hair and say, "Why do you look so pissed off? What, you can't look in the mirror at yourself without frowning? That's the only person you've got, that one in the mirror. *Smile*."

She was a native of Spain with the trademark Spanish fiery confidence. When she talked to you, she grabbed your attention as if it were a necktie. She told us how deeply she loved the ocean and the mountains and food and friends. The way she talked about the things she loved, it was easy to tell she had learned to love in a deep and unbridled way. I wished I could learn to love like that. She walked like a queen. She also liked philosophy and surfing, a pair of interests which resonated with me. She didn't smile too big or too much but still exuded happiness. The way she exuded her soul through her voice and actions was authentic and contagious.

I would do a pose that I thought went well. She would walk over and gently kick me and whisper "again" while lecturing everyone else about the difference between *mula bandha* and *uddiyana bandha*. I was still doing crazy things like drinking two hundred ounces of water a day and fasting way too much.

Even after a year of yoga, I still didn't know how to inhale deeply. I was too busy trying to look a certain way. Her feedback and criticism helped me see what kind of change I needed.

I listened to her podcast on identity. I'd never felt more disconnected from a concept. My identity for seven years had been "accommodating husband of controlling wife." More than two years had passed, but I was still clinging to the shadow of that identity. Now I was *divorced* accommodating husband of controlling wife. But I had forgiven her, right? So where did that leave me?

Had I forgiven myself? I did not know. I needed to find out.

I kept staring deeply into the Bikram mirrors and I kept writing. I poked around and found the perfect place to take writing breaks not far from the yoga studio. Dr. Bombay's Underwater Tea Party, in Decatur. Decatur is the creative center of Atlanta. It has the most bookstores, art studios, and diversity. Among the many places I stumbled into, Bombay's felt like home. The walls are lined with bookshelves and the ceiling is plastered with upside-down umbrellas. It breathes creativity and calm.

The first time I walked in I knew this Tea Party was meant for me. I sat down with my MacBook and picked up where I had left off in my manuscript.

Before long, a waiter brought me a menu.

"Hello! I don't recognize you," he said. "Have you been in before?"

"First time!" I answered. "Do you have any juice or salad?"

"This is a *tea* house," he responded. "We have a lot more to explore on our menu than juice or salad. You can go anywhere for that. Here, we do High Tea, Cream Tea, or just tea, and you can pick from our assortment of fresh baked scones or pastries with clotted cream, custard, and real butter. We source our teas from all over the world. They come with their own pot and one free refill. Since this is your first time, I'd recommend a cream tea with scones, and we can start you with a Jasmine Jazz and a Strawberry Vanilla. Sound good?"

At first, I cringed at the suggestion of so many sugar-based options. At the same time, I felt drawn to this place for a reason. I was already committed to trying new things. The plant-based snacks I had been making the boys in my dehydrator mostly

ended up down the garbage chute. If this place was pairing literature and tea, two things I already loved, with treats, maybe I
could trust it. Maybe added sugar wouldn't be so bad.

"When in Rome!" I caved. "Let's go for it. As far as palette
cleansers for later, do you have sorbet?"

"Oh no," he replied with a twinkle in his eye as he took my
menu and folded it under his arm. "Here, we only serve *real* ice
cream."

If this was going to be my new writing spot, I was going
to let go of my food control issues. I let my guard down and
got excited to have dessert for lunch. I was worthy of dessert.
I opened my MacBook and typed away as I eagerly awaited my
first private tea party.

I soon decided that not only were tea parties acceptable, but
I far preferred them to juice and salad. I took myself to tea parties and wrote for hours at least twice a week. All that sugar
brought me back to thinking about the highlights of my childhood, and what I could do to enrich the boys' childhoods. We
had a McDonald's a quarter mile from home, but I had never
gotten them a Happy Meal in their lives. I had been too afraid
of the preservatives. When I visited the Smithsonian in DC the
week of the eclipse, I saw a McDonald's hamburger on display
from like fifty years ago that looked as good as new. That image
haunted me ever since.

But the recent private book-writing tea parties shifted my
fear matrix. Now I was more afraid of living a miserable plant-
based life than of eating fast food. I trusted our bodies to do
their part of sorting through that mess. We started riding bikes
to get Happy Meals.

Part of the reason I wrote so much was to finish the manuscript before my Panama trip in February. I wanted to review

the whole thing with my mom during the trip. She was going through the book-writing process with me, and it was very hard for her. She opened up about the way her mother treated her poorly at different points in her life.

Mom had recently invited her mother to live with her instead of going to a care facility. She would follow Mom around the house saying how much she hated her. My dad finally said *enough*, and they were working to find her a care facility.

I wrote my parallel story about the trauma of my marriage and processed it with Mom; Mom opened up about her current trauma with her mom and processed it with me. I would write a few pages, then I would send them to Mom to read and give me feedback. Our conversations became deep and meaningful as we prepared for Panama.

My body had changed a lot after twelve months of Bikram with no weight training or other exercise, and a diet of juice and (now) scones. I was withering away. Suzanne and Diana, my Bikram teachers at home in Atlanta, were getting worried about me. I often stayed after class to help clean up, or just to chat.

"Matthew, I'm a little worried about you. I think you might enjoy branching into other types of yoga. Have you ever thought about Vinyasa?" asked Suzanne.

"No, I like it here. Bikram works for me," I said. "Why do you ask?"

"Well, I know the owner of some studios here, and they teach Vinyasa. It's lots of young people and builds strength. You're always welcome here but I think you'd really like it. The owner, Elise, used to be a concert pianist, and it might even be good for the two of you to date," said Suzanne.

The pilot light on my heart flickered a little bit. I had kept that flame off for a long time and was trying to keep it off for the three years on my vision board. It had been two years and change, but not three. Suzanne's statement sent my heart soaring. I knew as well as she did, I would absolutely try this other studio for the prospect of love. I would follow her advice and give my needs a little oxygen.

"Elise is divorced now. She and her husband started their studio together a few years ago," Suzanne continued. "I think they are still business partners. I don't know if she's dating again, but I bet she is. Just go to a class where she's the teacher. It's called Highland Yoga. They are on MindBody, just like us. Their flagship location is just up the road."

They also had a location walking distance from my condo, and Elise was teaching that afternoon. I bought a monthly membership and booked the class. I was nervous. I knew Vinyasa, found it easy and boring; nothing like the challenge of Bikram. But maybe I could do them back-to-back as a challenge. Maybe love was closer to me than I thought!

My heart beat like a hungry hummingbird as I went into Elise's class. I instantly knew who she was as I walked through the door. My yoga journey, from Jo-Lynn to Cleve to Suzanne to Elise, my destination, made sense. She was right here by my condo the entire time.

I had learned a little bit about yoga studio ownership. A husband and wife ran the three locations where I practiced yoga in Greenville. I thought about how nice it would be to have a poised and flexible spouse with whom to run a yoga studio. I took them to dinner and asked if they thought it was a good business opportunity. They said no! Owning a yoga studio was a terrible idea! The only money they made was from the merchandise they sold in the gift shop.

Now in Elise's lobby, I considered the possibility of experiencing that terrible idea with someone like Elise one day. I was approaching my three-year mark and wanted to plan for dating and relationships. I still felt out of place in Atlanta; it was so different from Utah where I had spent ninety percent of my life. Yet Atlanta looked like it would be my future. Karen had recently gotten engaged to Ron, a native of the South. I agreed in our divorce papers to move wherever Karen got a job after she graduated. It seemed I was stuck in Atlanta long-term. Getting to know Elise looked like a logical step toward a potential long-term solution.

It felt like fate.

She was the center of attention. As I placed my shoes and hoody in a cubby, I watched how graciously she dismissed the long line of guys who were there to vie for her attention. I realized how long it had been since I had spoken to a girl. Well over a year. I didn't remember how. So instead, I peacocked around in my skimpy yoga clothes to make sure she noticed me but said nothing. I already knew Suzanne had told her about me.

Her class was easy as I had expected. I still gauged things based on energy and performance rather than joy, and this was way easier than Bikram. The only hard part was the little core crushing sequence in the middle, but that went fast. I never once felt like I was going to die. In Bikram, it's not uncommon to feel like you are going to die several times in one session.

The best pose in both practices comes at the end. *Savasana*. Dead pose. You make your final movements, turn over onto your back, stretch out, and lay still and silent like you are dead. I used this time in Bikram to contemplate my mortality. That was part of why it helped so much with working through divorce. "If that yoga didn't kill me, divorce definitely won't!" and "Life feels so beautiful, just to be alive, just to be breathing," were the sorts of thoughts I had while in Bikram.

In this *savasana,* I thought of Elise. She brushed by me and whispered toward my ear, "Beautiful practice."

I tried not to smile until she took a few more steps. I failed. The smile broke ground right away. I took her whisper as validation to keep coming to easy yoga.

The Vinyasa practice was too short, too easy. I would either double-up and do two classes in a row or do Vinyasa and Bikram back-to-back.

I reported back to Suzanne that I had made contact with Elise.

"How did it go?" Suzanne asked.

"Well, the yoga is pretty boring, but she did compliment my practice. I think I'll keep going."

"Oh, that's great Matthew! Are you going to ask her out?"

"Well, I would like to," I stumbled, "but I haven't dated in a long time, and I don't want to come across as creepy. So many guys seem like they are there just to ask her out. I was thinking I'll practice for awhile and then ask her closer to Christmas. What do you think?"

"I don't think you need to wait that long," she said. "I already told her a little bit about you, and she seemed interested. I wouldn't drag it out. Just be patient because she is very busy. Let me know how it goes!"

As Christmas approached, I decided to take a few weeks off from work. This would mean kissing my monthly bonus goodbye for the first time in years. It was like my version of Catholic lent. I wanted to write and make some room for dates.

After a few more practices, a few more glances and whispers, I asked her if she wanted to get a juice after class. She politely declined because she had to go to a meeting but gave me her number and asked if we could some other time. A week later I asked again, and she said she was busy again, but invited me to practice with her in an advanced yoga class. I joined.

The advanced class was fun and challenging. The teacher was another woman, who paid a lot of attention to me during class. It felt like too much attention. I caught Elise in what looked to me like a jealous stare a couple of times. If these jealous glares were an opportunity for me to re-engage with Elise, I missed it. After I talked with the other yoga instructor after class, Elise was gone.

The next day went by, then a week, and I saw her in passing a few more times. She ignored me. She wasn't interested. Devastated though I was, this feedback helped me. I needed to not jump the gun on any relationship moves. I needed more time to ease myself back into life. I was two years into my healing process. One year to go. Things were improving. Time was flying. Rhett would finally start kindergarten. I would finally pay off my student loan. One more year and I would make it to 2020, when I knew everything would be better. I could feel it.

"Hey, Suzanne," I said after yoga during Christmas break. "Well, I took your advice and went for it!"

"Oh yeah? That's great! How did it go?"

"We texted a little, and she invited me to an advanced class with her, but after that I think she decided she wasn't interested."

"Oh, bummer," Suzanne commiserated. "Well, what do you think of the practice?"

"Yeah, it's okay, though it helped me realize I do need to have more fun! You are right that I have gotten way too serious about yoga and life and everything. The practice is different but fun, so I'll keep on for now."

"That's great!" said Suzanne. "I'm sorry it didn't work out with Elise, but I think that's so good that you are enjoying the yoga and branching out."

Branching out. I saw myself as a cold and withering tree that still needed more branching out. Panama was just around the corner. I had been talking to my youngest sister Lindsay about going with me back to New York, so we could explore our love of art and literature together. I surprised her with the May 2019 trip as a Christmas present.

I didn't want to wait five more months to see *Hamilton,* so I bought a ticket to the Fox Theater in Atlanta.

My third and final year of healing was going to be *fun.*

Photos

November 2016. Featured in this photo are the two people I spent the most time the first two years after divorce: my sister, "Auntie Kelly," and my oldest son, Rex. Like I mention in the Dedication, we found portals to adventure at each city intersection, including this one outside the Vortex in Little Five Points, Atlanta. This was their natural formation, rolling smoothly down select city sidewalks. To the delight of onlookers, yes, but never more than the delight to Rex (see Chapters 1–8).

February 2019. I spent my third year after divorce going inward. Fasting, yoga, meditation, and quiet time with loved ones. Here I'm sitting with my mom at the café on the cacao farm in Bastimento, Bocas del Toro, Panama. We came here for healing conversation, strolls spotting strawberry-red dart frogs on flower petals, pocket-Scrabble matches, and revitalizing foods like the lemongrass tea steeping in the pot on our table (see Chapter 9).

March 2020. Once my three years of divorce recovery were up, I knew change was coming. A few Reiki readings in late 2019 confirmed it: my soulmate was ready and waiting for me, and major change was coming for not just me but for the whole world. Featured in this picture, taken in Buckhead Atlanta, one week before Covid stopped the world and paved the way for me to head back west to Utah and Arizona, is a brand new Vanderhall Venice I rented to cruise with Auntie Kelly and several other relatives who came to visit for Rex's baptism. I'm wearing the "racing clothes" that don't have room for a wallet in Chapter 12. One year later, after getting pulled over for speeding in Arizona, I found out I'd been driving on a suspended license for six months. Apparently, since I was going so fast when ticketed in the Vanderhall, I'd gotten a Georgia Super Speeder ticket in the mail . . . one I never received, since I moved suddenly just a week later.

Chapter 9

PanaMama

MOM AND I WERE GOING TOTALLY OFF-GRID IN
Panama. Francesco had taught me how to balance work
and fun during our workdays in Miami, and I would honor
his wedding week by not working. My book was written, and
I didn't bring a laptop. I didn't buy an international phone plan.
We would have Wi-Fi periodically. It was time to unwind, relax,
and get to know my mom again.

I hadn't really hung out with her in over a decade. I graduated
high school and went straight to college. Straight from my first
year of college to my LDS mission. Straight from that to a seven-
year marriage that did not include her much. In the two years
since my divorce, other than when she first brought the boys
and I from Utah back to Georgia, we were around each other
only in group settings.

Prior to graduating high school, we did things together all
the time. While writing my book, we talked a lot more. I was
excited to go on some adventures in Panama with Mom.

After arriving in Bocas Town we quickly found our water taxi
between two restaurants at the water's edge. There were only a

few other people on the boat. On the ride, I pointed out Francesco's favorite restaurant. He said you can sit on the deck and watch stingrays swim by.

We could almost see our tree house from the main island. As the water taxi left Bocas, the little group of villas across the bay grew larger as I pointed them out.

"Mom, look, that's our place!" I shouted over the roar of the wind and the boat engine. "Just to the left of the closest point to us. There, that's it!"

No response.

I looked over at her and saw her smiling, speechless.

"So cool," she finally whispered in wonder and bliss.

I was a proud son in that moment.

My pride took a hit when we debarked to check into the tree house. It was a little outpost with half a dozen hotel rooms on stilts in the water, a restaurant, and a few other tree houses.

"We don't have any running water at the moment, from the drought," the owners said at check in. "The restaurant is temporarily closed, but we may open tonight if some food comes. Oh, and your tree house lost power yesterday, but we hope to have the electricity back on soon."

Mom didn't seem concerned. She and I had agreed in advance to dismiss our usual proclivities in exchange for jungle adventures. We had left for a week abroad with only a small backpack apiece.

The heaviest item in my bag was the fifty double-sided pages of computer paper, thick with humidity, that I had finished writing. Mom had already gone over a lot of it as I sent it to her in spurts over the previous six months.

The restaurant opened, and we ate coconut toast with jam every morning out on our private dock. The ocean breeze was rejuvenating. We read parts of my manuscript and played Scrabble as we sat out on the dock.

I opened up about my healing journey and all I was going through. She opened up about how difficult it was to put her mom in a nursing home. All their past difficulties had come to the surface.

"My mom didn't want me when I was born," she said. "She already had her kids, and she and my dad were going through a tough time. He was having an affair when I was born. I think if it wasn't for me, she probably would have left him. I was like a death sentence for her, because it meant she was stuck with him. She told me that she wished I would die. I don't blame her because that was her reality, and it was all she had to give to me. I think in the long run it was for the best they stuck together, but at the time it was awful. It was just awful."

I felt Mom's pain as she cried. I held her hand and listened.

"Since she didn't want me, my only purpose was to serve her. I was a big inconvenience to her, so if I didn't make her life better, I was worthless."

I was stunned by my mom's honesty and vulnerability. I had never heard about any of this before. I knew their relationship was hard, but I had no idea it was so severe. Mom had a strong sense of duty to her kids and thought she didn't do enough for us. She got a job as a college recruiter to offer us reduced tuition and hang out with us at high school. Everything she did was for her kids. I now saw that was because she wanted to be for us what her mom had never been for her.

"This sort of behavior was rampant on my side of the family," Mom said. "The men were predators and abusers, and the women were stuck with them. It's why there isn't much left from my family." They were fragmented and scattered, and never had reunions.

She was the definition of swimming upstream to save her children. Saving us was only part of the battle. How could she unlearn lies that were told to her repeatedly by her own mother during her most formative years? I knew how hard it was for me to try to unlearn the lies I told myself and others during a handful of adult years.

"I love you, Mom," I said. "Thank you for sharing that with me."

We had five days on the wild side of the island before going to the Red Frog Beach Island Resort for the wedding weekend. We kayaked, paddle boarded, and walked through the jungle beneath a canopy of howling monkeys. At night, the monkeys played around outside the windows of our treehouse. We walked to the cacao farm in the jungle for lunch and played Scrabble on their single dining table. We traversed the island to Merlin Beach to snorkel. Our cell phones stayed locked in a safe.

The treehouse half of our trip ended with a day at sea. After a day filled with starfish and dolphins, our boat driver took us a secluded beach late in the afternoon to relax the rest of the day away.

"You two go on in and I'll stay here," he said, chill as ever as he killed the engine about sixty feet from shore.

"Great! Can we leave our stuff with you?" I asked.

"Of course! Enjoy yourselves! There is the most marine life down there of any beach in Boca," he boasted.

"Great, see you in a little bit, thanks again!" I said, mirroring his excitement.

We grabbed our snorkel gear and plopped into the warm ocean water and swam ashore. No sooner had we stood on the beach than we heard the boat engine roar back to life. We turned around to see our phones and passports and transportation disappear. But that wasn't the only thing that threw us off.

The beach had one other occupant, who looked fine from a distance, but up close appeared menacing. On the beach, an iron sign mounted on a pole proclaimed, "This beach is a place where pirates come to steal things."

I walked past the man sitting on a fallen log to get a better look at him without staring. He wore a wide-brimmed leather hat. He wore several layers of loose-fitting leather clothing and had a few bags full of what I can only assume was loot from traveling snorkelers. A rusty old sword lay next to him on the log. Tattoos on his face and arms jumped out at me, including one that looked like a black spot on his wrist.

He seemed visibly disappointed in us, like we should have left our bags on the beach for him to pilfer through. We had nothing. What valuable things we did have were on the boat that had apparently abandoned us.

I had two important discussion points to address with my mom. One, we were abandoned on an island beach with no exit plan. Two, we were accompanied by a pirate who said nothing but kept staring.

Instead, I said, "Let's check out this reef!" We moved away from the pirate to get our snorkel gear on. When we returned, he was gone.

I went to explore the large concrete pipes and huge coral boulders on the ocean floor. I bobbed my head up every so often to examine the beach and check on my mom. She walked the shallows examining seashells. Then she was gone. I swam back to the beach and found her on a little raised outcropping covered in spiky green grass.

"He's still gone," she lamented of our boat captain, peering out at the waves. I plopped down next to her. "Do you think he's coming back?"

He had been gone for well over an hour, maybe two. It was nearing sunset, with limited time left before dark. Though the bay looked beautiful and triumphant in the fading orange light, it looked equally vast and defeating.

"Honestly, I do not know," I replied.

"Looks like a pretty far swim," Mom said. "Could we make it?"

We saw our treehouse off in the distance, probably around two miles away across the bay. Maybe half a mile out was the waterway where boats passed through every fifteen minutes or so. With night approaching, the boats were slowing.

"I honestly don't think we could make it to the other side," I replied, choosing honesty over reassurance. "But I do think we could make it to where the boats are passing and flag one down."

Mom laughed. "Can you imagine? 'Help us! SOS! Our boat-man left us out here to die!'"

"He hustled us and fed us to the pirates!" I added, laughing with her.

I shuddered at the thought of swimming toward the boats in the encroaching darkness. I shivered at the fear of being stranded here for the night.

And then I realized, even in the worst-case scenario, we would still be okay. On this secluded beach halfway across the continent, I had found a relationship with my mom that had been missing for ten years. We had shared parts of our hearts that felt cold and alone. As scary as our outer reality seemed, our inner selves were feeling seen and heard.

We called out over the ocean with whoops and hollers. Come what may, we would be okay.

I felt in that moment that I had finally found what I had searched for. Waited for. Yearned for. With everything stripped away from me, with nothing but the love of my mother between me and life and death, I found it. The peace and happiness I felt with my mom in that still moment on the destitute beach was exactly what I had been looking for.

In the spiky grass, I danced out our skit of hailing a rescue ship, when the unmistakable "glug, glug, glug" of our little boat came back into earshot. We whipped our heads around and stared at each other.

"It's him! It's him!" Mom exclaimed, then she started to cry. "It's really him."

She gave me a hug, and we walked down to the beach. He beached the boat and helped us on board.

"Where the heck did you go, man? Leaving us with no notice like that?" I yelled at our mutinous captain. "We didn't know if you were coming back!"

"Got hungry, man, it was dinner time," he replied. "The lunch spot was really busy, and I had to wait a long time." His French fries sat next to him in an open to-go box.

Mom and I huddled next to each other in the whipping cool air as we raced across the bay to the tree house, grateful for the boat that had returned to take us home.

We took our time getting ready to depart for the Red Frog on Sunday morning. We could have taken a water taxi but instead decided to walk across the island. We had inquired enough to know it was possible but hadn't met anyone who had done it. It was a long and disorienting hike. We met a few locals along the way who pointed us in the right direction. Later that night we met up with Francesco for dinner. After warm introductions, I told him about our journey.

"Wait, you walked across the whole island from Bastimento?" he asked, eyes wide.

"Yes, the trail got thin a few times, and we went the wrong way once, but we made it!"

"I have been here so many times, bro, but never heard of that," he said. "You guys are crazy!"

"This trip has already been an amazing journey for both of us," I said, motioning to Mom. "We are making the most of every chance we get! How has it been over here?"

"Bro, let me tell you, we have been living it up!" Francesco exclaimed with a trademark Panama finger snap. "We have half of this resort reserved and they treat us like royalty! Massages, free drinks, the meals are included. It was not cheap, but it was worth it!"

The villa was a mansion. We had a huge, glamorous room up the road from the beach, adjacent to Francesco and the rest of the wedding party. We scarcely entered the front door before Mom had the washing machine and the bathtub roaring to life. I was so proud of her roughing it with me in the tree house for a hundred hours, then walking across the island with me. Now, we enjoyed marble floors and spiral staircases and running water.

It was my first ever beach wedding. Francesco and his bride had been together for several years. In their vows they called each other "partners in crime." I loved that concept: sharing each other's deepest secrets, open and vulnerable, ride or die, for better or worse. That's how it was supposed to be. I desperately wanted that kind of love for myself. I believed if I kept to my vision board, in one year, I would be ready to find that, too.

Chapter 10

Pandy

TWO DAYS LATER, BACK HOME IN ATLANTA, I stepped onto my yoga mat and faced the mirrors in Suzanne's early Friday morning class. I smiled from ear to ear when I unexpectedly saw my real self looking back at me. I had spent almost a thousand hours glaring at myself in those mirrors. After a transformational vacation with Mom, I returned to see myself looking back at me. Misty, happy eyes looked back at me as I practiced that day. As I looked into my own eyes, with forgiveness and hope, I felt a powerful sense of newness flow through me.

It had been far longer than just since my divorce that I had seen the real me in the mirror. A memory surfaced from 2009 in the Kanab High School weight room. I had finished a workout with my brother Kyle, and we flexed in the mirror, making Arnold Schwarzenegger poses. That was the last time I could remember seeing the real me.

On my yoga mat I suddenly became that same young and eager kid.

I had scowled at myself in the Bikram mirror for the past year and a half. Judging myself. Hating myself. Seeing myself as a loser, a failure, a fraud.

A thousand teacher comments came to my mind.

"Why are you looking pissed off in the mirror? See yourself with gratitude."

"Move through the postures with no judgment, just be. Just breathe."

"Remember, yoga is a journey. We will never be perfect. Set realistic expectations for yourself."

"Breathe, breathe, breathe. Why aren't you breathing?"

I had spent three decades of my life basing my feelings on my performance. If I did a good job, I would feel good from the praise of others. I had carried that into yoga. I wanted to get every pose perfect every time. In Bikram, it's just not possible. The room is set to 105 degrees with forty percent humidity. Even when your mind and body are in sync and everything flows easily, it's never going to be perfect.

In that moment looking in the mirror, I felt like Robin Williams at his return as Peter Pan in *Hook*. The lost boys gather around him, and he kneels next to the smallest of them. The little boy removes Peter's glasses and looks him deep in his eyes. He touches his cheeks, plays with his face, and finally sees his old ageless friend, as if he were still a child.

"Oh, there you are, Peter!" says the little lost boy.

All the other boys come touch his face and rejoice at the return of their long-lost leader.

That was me. There I was. I finally saw what I was looking for.

As a toddler, I used to hide popcorn behind the couch for Peter Pan. I thought he would come at night and eat it. Other kids hid cookies for Santa, but I hid popcorn for Peter. I nicknamed myself "Pandy the Boy." Friends and family gave me a lot of nicknames over the years. But the one that came back to me the most, for my youthful exuberance and general disregard for rules, was always "Peter Pan."

I did not want to have a Wendy-Mother give me rules. I did not want to find a Wendy-Wife to hold me accountable for my lies or see me for the scared boy I was. I did not want to grow up and be a "man." I wanted to fly away whenever I could. I wanted to be my own self-proclaimed king of Neverland. Rollerblading all over cities with Rex on my shoulders, pulling all-nighters, breaking the rules. Did that mean I would never be a man? Could I not have fun and grow up at the same time?

I suddenly saw my problem clearly. Sure, I was back; now, I needed to grow. If I was going to find love in one year and be ready to rebuild my life on the foundation of an honest relationship with my partner, I needed to face these fears. No more doing things on the surface to make her happy, inwardly hiding my own needs and meeting them in secret, then resenting her for how that all turns out. How could I transform this immature egomaniac Peter Pan inside me into a devoted partner? I needed more help.

I sat down that night to take a serious inventory of myself and make plans for self-improvement. I titled four pages in my journal: spiritual, mental, emotional, and physical.

Physical. My body felt great overall from the yoga, but I had some stomach problems. I had long heard of acupuncture and wanted to try it. I had not only let go of my strict juice diet, but veered off in a new extreme, eating mostly desserts like what I got at Bombay's. Now that I was doing Vinyasa Yoga, I was interested in building strength again. Someone tipped me off to what a more challenging yoga called Ashtanga.

Work on diet: check.

Go to acupuncture: check.

Start building strength again: check.

Ashtanga yoga: check.

Mental. I had worked so hard on my book the last six months, and as much as it helped me process my feelings, I hated it. I felt like it wasn't good enough. I had long-term goals to become a published author. I needed to start somewhere.

Find book publisher: check.

Emotional. Sharing feelings with Mom helped. I was rebuilding my relationships with my siblings, too. I needed to keep doing that. I had New York City with my youngest sister Lindsay coming up at the end of May. I invited Mom to come visit me in Atlanta to hang out for a couple of days around my birthday. I would keep journaling, keep writing, and keep opening up. Give myself a few more months, and then take a leap and start dating in preparation to meet someone special.

Keep rebuilding family relationships: check.

Start dating by the end of summer: check.

Spiritual. This one was hard. My entire life I had been taught the Church had all the answers. I still believed that theory, but I recognized most of the healing I found was from other sources. Many of these sources were frowned upon or even condemned by the Church. That was confusing. I wanted to branch out further and see what spiritual guidance I could find. I heard about Reiki and wanted to try it, but it felt too woo-woo. Yoga was bridging the gap for me, but Reiki felt too distant. I would stay committed to church and trust that it would guide me. There were plenty of Eastern traditions I could explore without going too far.

Keep having faith and going to church: check.

Stay open-minded but don't go too far: check.

On a Friday in April when I didn't have the boys, I finished my morning meetings and walked a few miles down Peachtree Street to an acupuncture clinic. I filled out a questionnaire, sat in the lobby, and sat some more. My healer was late. I had cut my maximum allowed fast duration in half, but sitting in their lobby made the half hour at the end of a relatively easy forty-eight hour fast feel difficult. It smelled like lacquer and bleach. I got dizzy. I needed to go outside. I stood up and headed for the door. Just then, my doctor came in the door.

"Leaving so soon?" she asked. "My turn for you, come with me."

"Oh, I uh," I mumbled, still feeling dizzy. "You were pretty late so—"

She grabbed me by the arm and took me into one of the few suites down the hallway.

I was in a typical hybrid Midtown Atlanta high rise. The bottom floor was shops and restaurants, then offices above those, then floors four or five on up were condos.

I sat down and she floated around the room a little bit, giving me brief directions, then sat down in front of me and asked for my hands. She moved her hands around my fingers and wrists, pinching and pulling, feeling different joints, measuring my skin in some unquantified way I hadn't experienced before. She set my left hand down and held my right wrist in both her hands and listened to my arm. She tapped it, pinched it, tapped it some more, twisted it a little, flopped it up and down, all the time whispering little notes to herself. I sat and watched, mesmerized. I closed my eyes and tried to tune into what she was doing. I felt the blood vessels. I breathed deeply and imagined the air flowing into my arm to illuminate answers for her.

"You not eating good," she said. "What you eating?"

"I do a lot of fasting and eat a lot of dessert," I replied.

"Why you punish yourself like that?" she replied. "Why you white people fast like that? It's no good for you. Your body carry you around all day and take good care of you but you no take good care of it. No good! No more fasting! You eat three meals a day! Got it?"

"Got it!"

She nodded. "You so skinny." She pinched the skin around my wrist and lifted it toward the ceiling, showing how sallow and stretchy my skin had become. "Eat more!"

I nodded in determination. I could eat more.

"Next thing, why you eat so much spicy? Your intestines in big trouble, I feel it, I feel it in you."

When I did indulge in real food, I spiced the heck out of it to make it more filling. I went through a jug of sriracha a month. So *that* was the source of my newfound stomach problems.

Another truth I could not deny. No more spicy food.

"What you need," she continued, "are cool foods. I feel you, you hot, always hot hot hot," she said. "I know you are. Too much hot. No more ginger, no more cinnamon," which were literally spices I used on everything, "no more pepper. More salt, and cucumber, and Greek yogurt, you need cool. You too hot already; you need cool food. Otherwise, this will be big trouble for you!"

I didn't want "big trouble for you." I nodded again. Three meals, more food, cool food. Got it.

She returned my hand, lay me down on the little hospital bed in her office, and stuck some long and wispy needles into my midsection. Twenty minutes later she removed them and examined me. She put a hand on my flat and starving stomach like I was a pregnant woman ready for an ultrasound.

"You hold too much pain here," she said, pushing down on my stomach. "Too much judgment. Release it. Let it go. Don't hold this here. Bad for you. Yoga, meditate, Tai Chi. Do some Tai Chi. Qi Gong. Release your judgment. I worry about you, but you will be okay."

Truth four, release tummy judgment.

Leaving her office, I walked down Peachtree Street hungry, but not letting myself feel it. Congested, but not sure why. Self-conscious but unaware of the source.

When I walked back up Peachtree, I skipped. I had my answers. I walked straight to Shake Shack and got a burger, fries, and a chocolate truffle shake.

Chapter 11

Graduation

IT WAS TIME FOR RHETT TO GRADUATE FROM THE preschool that said he had autism. His graduation reminded me of the achievements I wished to enact in my own life. *Publish a book. Keep rebuilding relationships and learn to love myself. Start dating again. Find love.* In springtime two years earlier, we had finalized our divorce. Now with the newness of spring all around, I was finally starting to feel like myself again. It was a perfect time to take meaningful steps to accomplish my goals.

Mom had recently visited for my birthday. I took her to Bombay's.

"Check it out!" I said as we walked through the door to the umbrella ceiling and walls lined with books. "Pretty cool right?"

"Shut the front door!" Mom exclaimed with her signature phrase. "This is where you wrote your book?"

"Yeah, right there mostly." I motioned to my favorite table near the window. "Over scones and hibiscus tea!"

"That is too cool," she said, scanning the steampunk decor. "I could not think of a more perfect place to write a book."

Writing had given me time to reflect on my regrets as a parent. Most of them centered around Rhett. He was so young during the mess of our divorce and then ended up stuck at this prison preschool for two years. I was glad it was finally over.

Often when I dropped him off at school, the teacher needed to hold him so I could leave and go to work. He would cry, sometimes scream, hold onto me, and say, "No, Daddy, don't leave me!"

His attachment and abandonment issues filled me with guilt. I wondered how often he looked through the classroom window and wished he saw his mom or me coming to get him.

Rex, Rhett, and I arrived early on the day of Rhett's graduation. Rex and I sat in the bleachers near Karen and Ron. Since I brought the kids to the ceremony, she was taking them from there.

The students sang some songs, and the time came to give them diplomas. Rhett was right in the middle of the pack. He looked so cute in his fire engine red cap and gown. He came into view about four kids before it was his turn and started walking closer to the stage, waiting for his name to be called. When his name was called, he walked up the steps nervously and received his diploma. We clapped and cheered.

Then he looked for us, his face pale as oatmeal as his eyes darted around, wondering if we were there. In his mind, we were gone. We had left him there, abandoned, and didn't love him. That's what I saw in his face. Tears welled in his eyes. Even though I had seen him minutes before, and he knew we were there for his graduation, he thought we were gone.

I leapt to my feet and started screaming louder.

"Go, Rhett! I love you so much!" I yelled at the top of my lungs. Everyone around looked at me like, "Whoa, *Dad,* this isn't a football game," but I didn't care. Rhett saw me and smiled up at me. He saw the rest of us and waved broadly. His nervousness washed away, and he skipped happily back to his seat, beaming.

I didn't sit down. I was overcome with emotion. I went from jumping and shouting for Rhett and walked straight to the exit, bawling uncontrollably. I had spent over an hour with him, told him we would be there the whole time, checked on him before the ceremony began, and still he thought I had gone. I had failed him. Now he was a nervous and ungrounded kid who didn't believe his parents loved him.

I ran to my car and drove straight to the Highland Yoga by my condo. I didn't talk to anyone, didn't sign in, just took my mat straight to the front of the class and flowed hard and fast through sad and angry yoga. Tears streamed down my face the entire time.

I lay there in Savasana for a long time after. I let myself feel the failure. I let it seep in.

Poor Rhett.

He did not feel loved.

The one thing I most wanted for him, to feel loved and grounded, he did not have. He felt alone and nervous. I had never felt like such a failure. Just when I thought I was healing from all the pain of divorce, I faced this even greater pain.

The next week I met my sister, Lindsay, in New York City. For two and a half years, we had talked about seeing *Hamilton* together on Broadway. It was finally here. For her, it was the trip of a lifetime.

She dove right into the breakneck pace of the city. We met for dinner at an old library converted into a restaurant. We took Ubers and rented bikes and strolled city streets. Other than *Hamilton*, she wanted to visit the 9/11 Memorial, The Met on Central Park, and the Statue of Liberty. Everything was easy except for Lady Liberty because I hadn't gotten tickets in advance. But we would try our luck.

After the Memorial, we saw a hustler holding a sign for Statue of Liberty tours. There is one certified tour company and then a bunch of sketchy ones. The brunt of the content on the Statue website warns against buying tickets from hustlers like the one we now approached. But this might be my sister's only shot, so I decided to try anyway. I would use a credit card, and if the tickets were no good, immediately get the charge reversed. We had already seen *Hamilton* and been to the Met, and we had all afternoon, so it was worth a shot.

"Are these real tickets?" I asked. "Don't worry, I won't judge you, it's just my sister really wants to see the Statue and we only have about eight hours until we need to go back to JFK."

"Yeah, of course, you got here right in time, the ferry picks up right over there, I can have my friend come give you a ride," she said, lying through her teeth as I stared at her fake Jordans. Everything she said sounded like a lie. I knew there was no "friend," knew there was no "right in time," but I wanted to believe it anyway.

"Okay, just swipe my card," I said. "Now, where do we board the ferry?"

"Go to that street corner and we will be there in five minutes," she said, motioning to a nearby streetlight. "The ferry leaves at two p.m., so that gives us just enough time."

Maybe we could pull this off. "Okay, thank you," I said. "And, if you're lying, I forgive you."

She walked away. I wondered if I had been hustled, but I also didn't want to know.

Her friend showed up at the street corner in like fifteen seconds.

"Hey, so y'all need directions to the ferry?" he asked.

"No, we are supposed to get a ride," I responded.

"Ha, well, I can't carry you, but it's about ten blocks straight down, straight to the docks from Freedom Tower. It leaves at two, so you better hurry."

I checked my phone. One forty-five p.m. We had a chance. But was the ferry real?

"Look, man, you can tell me the truth," I said. "Is there really a boat?"

"Hell, yeah, man!" he said, laughing at my indecision. "Get running!"

Lindsay and I had our luggage for the airport. I had Lindsay hand me her bag and reviewed the plan.

"Okay, Linds, honestly, I think this is a scam," I told her, already thinking of reversing the hundred-and-eighty-dollar charge on my Amazon card if need be. "But we have a chance. I believe there is a boat. I believe I can get there with both bags and you can get there too. What do you want to do?"

"Let's go for it," she said. "No regrets!"

And with a chuckle, we were off.

I galloped down the street like a packhorse with our luggage, looking back at Lindsay and cheering her on. What an adventure.

We reached Freedom Tower in no time and turned left toward the Hudson. Lindsay was maybe a block and a half behind me. I reached the river and saw the boat! It was huge, a lot bigger than the official tour boat I had taken with Rex and Kelly a couple years earlier. I picked up speed and reached the ticket counter at one fifty-eight p.m.

"I have tickets!" I yelled, exasperated. "Can we get on?"

I looked back to see Lindsay running like the wind, having just reached the wide sidewalk along the Hudson. We were gonna make it!

"Sir, these are vouchers to get tickets, you still need to go online and reserve a time. Do you see these people in line here?"

I looked past him and saw probably two thousand people in line.

"Even after you reserve a time, you have to wait in line."

I didn't argue. We had been hustled. I walked back to Lindsay and gave her the news.

"Well, at least we tried," she said.

We walked down a boardwalk for a water break and for me to call Chase and reverse the charge. Lindsay learned more about me in those thirty minutes than she may have learned her whole life. Impulsive, optimistic, wild.

While on the phone with Chase, I climbed a concrete railing and hopped over to a few pillars in the river. I came back to Lindsay as I hung up, only to be greeted by two very perturbed-looking police officers.

"Sir, do you realize you have created a safety hazard by climbing that wall and playing monkey over there?" the leader cop said in a thick New York accent.

"Hello, officer, no, I did not realize that," I said in my usual cheeky manner.

"I'm going to need to see some ID," he continued.

No way I was giving him that. With my sister standing next to me and having just vanquished the Statue scammers while also getting in some great cardio, I pled my case.

"Officer, I am sorry to cause any trouble. We are visiting town and are about to leave, and I saw no sign saying not to climb. May we kindly depart with a warning?"

"Sir, it's a wall." The officer motioned at the structure. "You don't need a sign where there's a wall, everybody knows you don't climb walls."

I stood silent.

"Now I'm gonna need that ID."

I held firm. "Officer, I will leave the area right now, I am sorry for any trouble. Now, will you please let my sister and me go?"

I looked at Lindsay to get mercy from this wall-protector and his silent companion. He looked back at his partner, who nodded, and then back at me.

"Get outta here," he said, with a classic New York dismissive arm wave.

Lindsay jabbed at me while we walked to Chinatown, imitating her best NYPD accent. "Sir, there's a wall, you don't need a sign where there's a wall!"

We wouldn't have enjoyed the Statue failure had it not been for the forty hours of bonding that preceded it. We walked Central Park and enjoyed the Obelisk and other unique expressions that bespeckle that icon of American love and creativity.

We basked in the glory of humanity at the Met and bawled at the rags-to-riches story they sang in *Hamilton*. The person sitting next to me belted the lines from *Hamilton* word-for-word, far too loudly. People were looking. I did him a favor.

"Your singing is great!" I whispered. "But do you think you could turn it down a couple of notches? I think it's a little hard for some people to hear the actors."

"Oh, yeah, I am sorry!" He responded loudly. He seemed about the same age as my sister, early twenties, and by himself. "I listen to *Hamilton* every night in bed before I go to sleep and have memorized the entire play. I love it! Sorry!"

Lindsay had returned home several months earlier from her

LDS mission in Tacoma, Washington, Spanish-speaking. Our Airbnb had a Mexican restaurant in the basement, and I loved hearing Lindsay interact with the staff in Spanish. I loved how she said "horchata" and other words. She sounded authentic. I could tell she was just as sad and awkward coming off her mission as I had been coming off mine years ago.

As we walked and talked, she cried and we hugged. We decided to have scripture studies on the phone together once a week, and for my next birthday in 2020, we'd go to Mexico. It helps the post-mission adjustment to have something to look forward to. I was glad to be a part of that for Lindsay.

We made many memorable stops in New York City. My favorite was Alice's Tea Cup on the Upper West Side of Central Park. I had been Insta-stalking them for months while writing at Bombay's. Their setup looked equally magical. Sprinkles and whipped cream were my thing, and they had them aplenty. I made our reservation for high tea several weeks in advance to make sure we had a spot.

High tea reminded me of Scotland with Dad. It reminded me of identity and truth, reminded me of writing again. Tea houses became my magical little escape from the world. I could withdraw from my raucous and rigorous sales career that took me so far out of myself and go within.

At Alice's Tea Cup, the hostess was dressed like Tinkerbell from *Peter Pan*. We walked down into the basement parlor to see her dusting patrons with pixie dust after encouraging them to make a wish. The magical sparkling dust glistened down through the air and fell on their outstretched arms and fingers as Tink flicked her wide powder brush at them. This was the end of the meal ritual! Make a wish with pixie dust!

After our tea, Lindsay and I, hopped up on sugar and carbs, pranced up to the counter for our sparkling coronations. We smiled with gleeful imagination as Tinkerbell whispered, "Make a wish!" and flicked strokes of pixie dust over us.

Our eyes were closed, arms outstretched in front of us, playing invisible pianos in the sky to make our fingers vibrate like the sprinkles in the air. I wished for someone to publish my book. I wished for it right there in a tea house that felt as magical as the one where I had written it.

That same month, I met two people who would help me work toward my goals—Hollis and Marsha. I was searching for help. Every day I read blog posts, wrote, and sent email requests to anyone whose contact information might be relevant to publishing my memoir.

A successful memoir writer from Atlanta kept coming up: Hollis Gillespie. She specialized in the same sort of book I had written. I emailed her a few times and subscribed to her newsletter. I got a few canned responses but couldn't reach her.

The address on her website was close enough for me to drive to. I saw an open-concept apartment complex with some industrial space. I knocked on the door of what looked like a business suite. Nobody answered, but the door was open, so I peeked inside and hollered hello. I saw a warm and inviting space inside, with a couple chairs and a table with some writing materials on top where I figured she must do writing consultations. As I looked around, she walked out, in pajamas.

"Hey, what are you doing here?" she asked, alarmed but not angry.

"Hi, are you Hollis?" I asked. "I just came to see if I could hire you to help me publish my book. I've been on your Shocking

Real Life website and I have a memoir, too, I need..." I trailed off
as I realized from her body language this was not Hollis. I also
realized that I was in someone's house. Not a writing studio.

"This is my home," not-Hollis said. "She's using this address
on her website? I hosted one of her workshops one time, and
this is how she thanks me? Figures!"

I jumped into action to harvest what I could out of a tight
spot.

"I am so sorry!" I said. "It was probably an old, expired web-
page or something, I tend to look before I leap, and this is my
fault! Here I am about to pop into your kitchen unannounced.
Love the plants, though, and what you've done with the place."

She warmed up. "When you do find Hollis, tell her I said
hello. And not to use my address."

"Haha of course," I replied. "Thank you!" We exchanged a
smile and said goodbye.

I emailed Hollis again, this time telling her the funny story,
again including a snippet of my memoir.

Hollis emailed me back and said she would read my manuscript. We set a meeting date for Sunday at Bombay's, the venue
where I had written most of the book.

Getting the meeting with Hollis spurred me to move forward
and visit an Ashtanga *shala*. Regular yoga happens in a studio.
Ashtanga yoga, I learned, happens in a shala. It's more sacred,
kind of like a temple. You leave your shoes and your judgments
in the lobby, and when you walk into the yoga room, you enter a
place of breathing and healing. The practice is largely silent and
deeply rooted in Hindu tradition. They chant in Sanskrit at the
beginning and the end of the practice. The practice is built on
five-second inhales and exhales. The more I read about it, the
more I knew I needed it.

I only found two shalas in Atlanta. I visited their websites and read teacher bios. Marsha's shala felt like home before I ever visited. I read her story and saw pictures of her and Kathy on the Balance Yoga website. Their smiles were authentic.

I pictured myself living a life free from judgment. My heart still felt heavy and closed. Yoga had brought me a long way in my process of stripping down and cleaning house. After two years of that I was finally in building mode. Ashtanga looked like it held the answers for building my foundation.

When I Googled "Ashtanga," the top video was from the most beautiful yogi I had ever seen, Laruga Glaser. She was coming to Balance Yoga for a workshop the same weekend I booked my consultation with Hollis. It was meant to be. I booked a month of classes, a spot at the Laruga workshop, and emailed Marsha to make sure I dressed appropriately and came prepared to my first class.

I went to my first Ashtanga practice on Thursday, April 25th, the day before Laruga arrived and four days before my meeting with Hollis. I needed my heart to be open before I met Hollis.

According to Google Earth I could save half a mile's walk by climbing a fence behind the shala next to the Emory University bus parking lot. I scaled the fence and dropped into the alley behind the shala just before the Laruga workshop started. I didn't realize the front of the room was a floor-to-ceiling window. Everyone inside saw me drop to the cement and dart away.

"That must be the new guy," Marsha said to instant laughter from her class, and then walked around to the lobby to greet me.

"Nice parkour moves!" Marsha said as I entered. "Nobody has ever come to class that way before!"

Marsha had already drawn me in. She exuded intelligence, calm, humor, acceptance, confidence, and commitment to yoga. Her dark brown eyes were kind, encouraging, enthusiastic, empowering. I had never felt so much enthusiasm from someone just from seeing their eyes. Without her enthusiasm, and without Kathy's encouragement, I would not have held the space to continue with my clumsy and shallow infant Ashtanga practice.

Kathy was a little taller than Marsha, with the same love and encouragement shining through her emerald-green eyes framed with long and beautiful red hair. I have never met anyone who smiled as much as Kathy. Her smile was healing. Even as months went by and I continued to hold tension in my shoulders and continued to breathe shallow breaths, she never got frustrated with me or judged me. She just encouraged me along.

Laruga's workshop was about gratitude, breath work, and invisible muscles around your core called *bandhas*. They were under and beneath the stomach, the same place the acupuncturist told me I held pain and judgment. The same place where I had first burst into tears while holding a camel pose in my first Bikram class eighteen months ago.

Was it finally time to let go of the pain?

As I practiced, I focused more on looking good than on following instructions. I was still controlling my breath rather than following it. Holding tension in each little muscle rather than trusting my core strength.

"It's okay!" said Kathy, trying to walk me through a sun salutation where I kept moving without breathing. "I've been doing this for years, and it's always a learning experience. Just keep breathing. Breath leads movement."

I felt so much love and care from Kathy and Marsha in those early weeks. They twisted my wrists and stood on top of my feet and helped me stop judging and start sliding into the practice.

Kathy touched my shoulders often, reminding me to release the tension I was holding there.

After the first practice, I felt a mixture of defeat and desire. This was the yoga for the few, the uncommon, the ones truly determined to be free. My image of being "good" at yoga and "athletic" enough for anything was shattered. If I was going to become an Ashtangi, I would need to release my judgment of myself and my need to be "good enough" or "better than." I didn't yet know how to sit in an uncomfortable place and be okay with it. But now for the first time in my life, I was willing to try. I went back to Vinyasa harder than ever for the next few weeks, feeding my ego with something I was good at, but soon I saw that the Ashtanga shala was the place for me. I canceled my other memberships and committed to Ashtanga exclusively.

Eight yoga classes and two nights later, I pulled up to Doctor Bombay's Underwater Tea Party and sat at the patio table I had reserved for Hollis and myself. I was so excited! Had she read my manuscript? Would she want to help? Would she think it sucked and I was hopeless? I had prayed and planned for an open heart to whatever she suggested. I walked around front and there she was.

"You must be Hollis," I exclaimed.

"Matt?" She took a step back and sized me up with shock and surprise. "You're Matt? Good Lord, I pictured an older gentleman with a bowtie and a cane. What's a dish like you doing meeting me at a place like this?"

I laughed. "Hollis, I have not learned much in my life, but I have learned the value of good tea. This is where I came to write most of my book. Thanks for coming."

I opened the door and motioned her inside. Hollis carried the air of a marine sergeant. She was of slight build but focused, and with classy horn-rimmed glasses that dared you to question her. She carried the class and composure of someone who knew exactly who she was and what she could do for you. Her hair was done up perfectly in place, like the tight little cornucopia of baked goods we were about to eat together. She walked intently and excitedly. I knew immediately she was the writing teacher for me.

We sat down and talked about my manuscript.

"The story, it's about a girl, what is that all about?" she asked me.

"It's the best I could do," I told her. "I couldn't write my actual story, and I felt like a connection to the feminine helped me heal from my marriage and divorce. I felt like the woman in my marriage, I was the feminine partner, the one doing most of the cleaning and the caretaking, and writing through the eyes of a woman helped me get it out."

As I explained my story to Hollis, I gained power where I used to feel paralyzed and embarrassed. I was finally speaking my truth.

I told her my story. A divorced dad to two divorced kids, I had pretended to have an affair, which came close to being a real affair. I betrayed myself time and time again in my marriage. I could admit these things now after writing about them.

"It's crap, isn't it?" I placed my hands on the table and leaned toward Hollis, who sipped on dandelion tea. "Tell me how to write it, Hollis, tell me. I'm ready!"

I asked her exactly what she wanted to hear. I asked a writer to tell me how to write.

She set her teacup down on the table and leaned toward me excitedly.

"Every story is the same," she started while I took notes. "Think about it. Ever notice how all books are about two hundred and fifty pages? Except *Harry Potter,* but not all of us can be J. K. Rowling. Tell me your favorite Disney movie. *Little Mermaid*? I love that one too," she said before I had a chance to interject. "The first twenty-thousand words, you introduce the character and their dilemma. Then, at twenty-thousand words, they meet a guide. Aladdin, take Aladdin. He's a street rat who goes to jail and then he meets Jafar in disguise, the guide. They always meet a guide. Then you get the middle of the book, the next forty-thousand words, to develop the plot. You have the ups and downs, and then BOOM! Sixty-thousand words, all is lost. The all-is-lost moment is crucial to the story. This is what makes or breaks your story. If you can get your reader to sixty-thousand, you break their heart."

I was rich soil for the writing seeds that Hollis planted. I compared those notes to what I knew of my manuscript. The whole thing was forty-thousand words, a hundred and forty pages, and it took me six months to write. I needed to do double the work in a fraction of the time. I was ready. I could picture the moments, I could see the structure, and it all rang true.

"Then," Hollis concluded, "you tie it together. You save it. You end it. You get twenty-thousand last words to end it. That," she clapped her hands, "is how you tell a story."

"Deal," I replied. "Hollis, I will write my story for you in eighty thousand words in one month if you will help me publish it. How does your fee structure work?"

"A month? No way, take your time," she replied. "And me? Don't worry about it, this is on me. I like doing this. We will get you published. I feel your energy and I want to be a part of it. I'll have you come speak at my writing workshop this fall. I will help you. I'll send you pitch letter examples.

"Once you're done, we pitch it out and get you a publisher. The industry is brilliant because you don't need to do any editing, you pick your best section and pitch it out. They will do the editing, change the names, they have their own way of doing that. What we need to do is sell your story. And that is where I come in. I have gotten people more book deals than I can count. You have a story to tell, and we will get it told. You'll need a publisher who specializes in memoirs with religious undertones, and this stuff is hot right now. We will get you a deal."

She stood up and we said our goodbyes. Hollis was off to another engagement. I had work to do. I drove straight home and started rewriting my story. It flowed. I cried. I wrote truthfully about the times I betrayed myself, the times I cut out my family and friends, and the lies I told myself to save my marriage instead of admitting the truth about it.

I cried and I screamed, and I called people and apologized and told them I loved them.

That day was Sunday, April 28th. I finished writing on Wednesday, May 15th, eighteen days later. I was working at the time in four different cities across the South and wrote most of it in Ubers, airplanes, and hotel rooms. I wrote every spare moment I had during those eighteen days. I could crank out a thousand words an hour when I got in the zone, and I had several five-thousand-word sittings. Eighty-four-thousand words in total. Two hundred and eighty pages.

I sent it to Hollis, and she replied, "Holy shit!"

I sent copies to friends and family to get feedback and check for accuracy. Hollis wrote a pitch email and sent a section of the book to several publishers. I was on my way to becoming a published author. I hadn't published anything since college, and none of that was about me, just news assignments for class. I hadn't published anything authentic since high school.

Two years of practice and one hour of Hollis had me back in the writer's chair. She had told me something she read in a

T.S. Eliot poem when she studied at Oxford: "April is the cruelest month." In April, all the frozen parts of the Northern Hemisphere must thaw and come back to life. They are used to being frozen, and coming to life again nearly kills them, but when they do, they bloom. That, she told me on the second-to-last day of April 2019, was what I was experiencing.

We met a handful of times over the next five months as we looked for a publisher. Hollis let me buy her lunches, but never let me pay her for her work. She had a writing workshop coming up in the fall, and she asked me to be her guest of honor. She believed we could have a book deal by then. I set my intentions in line with hers. By October I would have a publisher.

Chapter 12

Mother Mary's Miracle and the Mintakan Mermaid

WHEN BEKA, A REIKI MASTER, WALKED INTO MY apartment, the energy she brought was so strong it felt like the windows would shatter. I got dizzy, the room spun like it was in a whirlwind, and my face became hot. I felt overwhelmed and tongue-tied at the unexplainable surge of energy that came in with her. Was this normal for her?

"Whoa," I laughed sheepishly. "Not sure what is happening, but I promise it wasn't like this before you got here."

"Yeah, I get that a lot," said Beka, calming my nerves. "Don't worry. Do you have a place we can sit and do some breathing to ground ourselves?"

We sat on my Ikea floor cushions and just breathed. I felt like I was coming back into my body. While we breathed, Beka prepared me for the session. She explained that while this amount of energy was unusual, it was a good sign that we would uncover some important messages. I had secretly wondered if the energy was due to her being attracted to me. I felt kind of embarrassed to learn it was not, but also excited that the energy meant we would uncover something meaningful.

Acupuncture six months earlier had so enlightened me that I proceeded to try everything Eastern. Anything connected to the ancient healing arts. I felt these disciplines were better for my soul than a New Age church or counseling.

Ashtanga Yoga had further opened my heart to the power of Eastern healing traditions. I had finally learned to see and love myself through this challenging discipline of breathing and moving. I memorized the primary and secondary Ashtanga series of movements and practiced for over an hour every day. I played sports again, got reflexology on my feet once a week, went to deep neuromuscular therapy once a month, had private yoga sessions with Marsha and Kathy to work deeper on my bandhas every six weeks, kundalini at an ayurvedic place around the corner from my condo, sound baths, cryotherapy, infrared therapy, chakra therapy, and going deep into private and guided meditation. Anything I could get my hands on. I was healing and loving it. I felt massive changes happening in my mind and body.

The more research I did, the more I came across Reiki. I was closed off to it at first, thinking it was too extreme, but the more I read the more I became convinced.

Reiki practitioners move the energy around your body and help you discover blockages to set them free. Poking around on social media, I found Beka on Instagram. She had healed herself from a terrible illness and now shared that gift with others. I felt her energy as I read her story and her posts. She was perfect. I needed a major shift, and I hoped she could help me create it.

For several months now I had been seeing the words "Picture your dream life" everywhere. I could not ignore it. The universe was ready for me to break free. But how? Karen was engaged to Ron, and I was tethered to her for the boys' sake. How could I manifest my dream life while making sure I stayed with the boys?

Karen had final decision-making, Karen was marrying a guy from the South, Karen would soon graduate with her PhD. She had the power to move us to any city she wanted. I had agreed to come along and pay for it. She would get her four thousand dollars a month until next summer, and then it would go to three thousand a month until the kids turned eighteen.

This was my reality.

Or was it?

Part of me knew I could manifest the life I wanted if I stopped blaming and finding excuses and just went for it. My dream life. But I did not know how.

I viewed the publication of my first book as representing my commitment to break free. Unfortunately, the pitches Hollis helped me write over the summer had fallen flat. We were approaching fall 2019, and I wanted to back out of the book altogether, to give up and abandon the project. If I published this memoir of our marriage, Karen would lose her mind. I worried that she would take it out on the boys. I had decided to stop trying to publish.

Yet inside I was screaming for independence. *Publish the book! Find your voice! Manifest your dream life! Move back West! Find a wife! Stop whining and finding excuses! Start loving yourself and make a home and a life where you can be the primary caregiver to your boys. Take a leap of faith and then watch it all happen.*

A higher voice spoke to that part of me. *You are not alone,* it reminded me. *Take the first step and then watch while I, the Universe, grant your wishes. All I need is for you to take that first step of faith.*

I didn't want to fight myself like this anymore. To be torn between what I really wanted and believed and how I chose to act. For ten years I had sacrificed myself to make Karen happy.

That kind of effort takes its toll. The subliminal message of me trying to make Karen happy was that I was not worthy of love. I was full of doubt and fear.

Ten years from the day when I first met Karen, Beka walked into my condo with her Reiki table. I would lay on my back so she could discover where my energy was blocked and help me remove them.

Before the energy work, Beka laid out Oracle Cards. They came in a little box with a book that explained what they meant. She carefully fanned them out in an arch between us, so that part of the back of each card was showing. After she spread them out, she asked me to say a prayer that I would find a card with a unique message for me. I really wanted to get the right message, so I spoke with deep intention. She followed with some insightful words of her own. She asked me to close my eyes and move my hands over the cards until I felt impressed to pick one up. My palm felt like it got hot over one of the cards. With my eyes still closed, I lowered my hand until I felt the edges of the card. I carefully slid it out from between the other cards and reached forward to hand it to Beka.

I opened my eyes as she showed me the card.

I accepted the card reverently with both hands. It showed a motherly figure in robes and read, "Mother Mary: Expect a Miracle."

I choked on the words at the bottom of the card as I read out loud, "Have faith that your prayers have been heard and are being answered."

I looked back at Beka, realizing I hadn't yet leveled with her about how stuck I felt in my situation. That was why she was here. I truly needed a miracle. Her card told me that I would have a miracle.

Beka smiled and read the card description. "Faith is the light that illuminates your pathway," she read. "Take whatever steps are necessary to keep your mind and heart filled with faith . . . Don't give up on yourself . . . That one small inkling of hope can eradicate the darkness of despair. Be the light . . . for as you make others stronger, it strengthens not only yourself but the entire world."

"Wow," I responded quietly with the only word I could muster. I knew in that moment I needed to publish my first book. That was my first step of believing in myself. Being the light. Lifting others.

Changing the world.

"You have a huge shift coming in your life," Beka lifted her gaze up from the Oracle book as she continued. "Everything is about to change. You are going to move, you are going to fall in love, and she is already there waiting for you. Does any of that resonate?"

"Um." I coughed weakly and nervously. "I wrote a vision timeline three years ago that this year I wanted to fall in love. As for the moving, yeah, I would like to. And yeah, overall, there is a lot I have been holding myself back from."

How does she know all of this? I wondered in amazement. *Clearly, she is getting stuff that is not written on the card. This is kind of unbelievable. But I believe!*

"Miracles are coming, Matt," she smiled. "When Mother Mary shows up, the Mother of God, miracles happen. I am so happy for you, and to see how this unfolds!"

Beka explained that she was also an empath. The truth was kind of easy for her because she could *feel* it. The universe spoke, and she listened. It whispered to her heart many of the things I was wanting to hope for but not yet willing to talk about.

I had been stuck in the darkness of self-doubt. *What if I wasn't ready? What if I was stuck in Atlanta for the rest of my life? What if Karen made us move somewhere even worse?* All these excuses sounded weak as they moved through my mind. The love and freedom Beka shared with me through Mother Mary sounded so much better.

My heart leapt as I dared to believe I was headed for love. I didn't know how. But I believed. That belief helped me to step into the light.

Beka moved me to the energy work part. She set up her table and had me lay on my back. Although I had felt melting hot minutes earlier, now I shivered and felt icy cold. She put a yoga blanket on me. She dangled a crystal, and it swirled over my chakras, my energy centers, as she moved it from my core up to my crown. I watched as it swirled gently around my abdomen, stomach, and heart. It hung deathly still when it reached my throat. I was in and out of meditation while she worked, but I saw the crystal sit very still as she dangled it over my throat. I knew what that meant. My voice was broken. The energy in my throat was trapped. I was stifling my voice. I was so afraid of letting the boys down, so afraid of letting Karen down, so afraid of failure, that I was sacrificing my voice. The culmination of two and a half years of writing and searching, was going to lie flat under the rest of the files in my laptop because I was afraid to set it free.

Not anymore.

Beka and I talked more after the session. I told her about the book, about my desire to move back home, about the complicating factors in my life with divorce and custody. I still judged myself harshly for being divorced. It was difficult to tell a peer in conversation that I was divorced. She held no judgment.

"Just go for it," Beka encouraged me. "The universe is on your side. What's more powerful than the universe? Take one step, and then another, and another. See where it leads you."

Just go for it. How simple. I knew she was right.

I decided that day, October 1, 2019, to publish my book no matter the cost. If I couldn't get a publisher, I would publish it myself. If it cost thousands of dollars to do and I never sold a single copy, it was still worth it. I had wanted to write and publish books my whole life. Here I had finally written a real book, a powerful memoir that could benefit countless people, and I was trying to sabotage myself into burying it. No more! No more stifling my voice to try to keep other people happy. The blockage in my throat was hurting my entire body and soul. I needed to be heard. I needed to find my voice. I needed to express myself. It was time to be loud.

After Beka left, I pulled out my laptop and began writing my second book. I realized I had a lot more to say than was in the first book. I believed the stories of my mistakes could help other people. I had no idea where book two ended, because I was still writing it in my life. Book two wasn't over yet. I needed to write it into existence. I needed to take some massive leap of faith and see where I landed.

I didn't know the ending, but I knew where it began. It began with truth. Just like my first book began with lies, this next book began with truth. It began with the truth and vulnerability of being divorced and LDS and feeling absolutely devastated. This was my reality that seemed impossible to reconcile. I thought of Mother Mary's son Jesus, the great reconciler, and believed that if I started writing the healing would come.

I needed to see where the truth would get me.

I closed my eyes as I wrote and imagined this dream life Mother Mary encouraged me to manifest.

It was warm; there were palm trees. I had a big bathtub, and a beautiful wife to drink tea with and study ancient texts and go to the beach. We smiled and cried and were real with each other. Where was I, I wondered? Then I saw it. I was in Phoenix, Arizona. My brother was in Phoenix for his MBA. I was already going to visit him at the end of October, in just under a month, to take him to the Arizona Cardinals game on Halloween for our annual bros trip. Phoenix was close to my other family in Utah, was a major city where I could probably still be a VP for Imaca, and was only a day away from the ocean. It was warm and had palm trees and a strong LDS community where I could find the partner I was looking for.

I imagined my life with boldness. It felt so good. It was the life I wanted, and I believed that by wanting it, it was already mine.

I fell to my knees right there in my living room. I prayed out loud, pouring out my heart to God and myself, and prepared to step into my dream. I knew on paper it was impossible: Karen was engaged, and we were stuck in Georgia. I had secondary custody of my kids. I had agreed in our divorce to move where *she* wanted to. Knowing this, I still believed, and prepared for my dreams to come true. I believed in a miracle.

Mother Mary had plans for me. Beginning that day, I kept her in my heart.

I called my mom more often to talk about my second book. I smiled and dreamed more often. Everything felt possible. I still didn't know how. I didn't need to.

Hollis had emailed me a few times about her writing retreat in two weeks at a mansion in the middle of nowhere, Georgia.

She had invited me to attend free of charge as her "guest of honor." I had dragged my feet on responding. Now I saw this as an important step toward publishing my first book. I emailed her confirming I would be there. Everything started to feel possible.

In the short weeks between Reiki with Beka and the writing retreat with Hollis, I got a response from one of the queries. The publisher asked for my first three chapters. I sent them. Taking this next step gave me more confidence that I deserved to have a voice.

The second night of the retreat with Hollis, on Saturday, October 19, at 11:54 p.m., I was offered a book deal from WiDo Publishing, the same folks who asked for the first three chapters. I was ecstatic. I left a note on the counter for the others and left at five a.m. Sunday morning to make it home in time for church. I was going to be published! When I got home, I sent WiDo my full manuscript. Ten days later, their Submissions Editor began an email to me with the following:

"Matt, I heard back from our Managing Editor today about your submission. She had this to say about it:

"This is the kind of LDS novel discriminating readers have been waiting to read. I couldn't put it down. Alternately heart breaking and laugh out loud hilarious, yet completely authentic in the portrayal of many struggles faithful LDS experience and prefer not to discuss. We'd love to publish it."

She understood my struggle! I felt validated. My voice rang out, and someone heard me! According to her, many others would want to hear me too. I broke down in healing tears. Salty tears of gratitude streamed down my cheeks and into the corners of my mouth. It felt so good to be heard. It made my circumstances a lot less scary.

I felt so grateful for Hollis! So grateful for Marsha! So grateful for Beka! So so so so grateful. I had taken small steps into the dark, and the universe brought into that darkness these beings of light who guided me along. I cried those grateful tears for a while. I had a lot of tears.

I asked Hollis if I should take their deal or keep shopping. The day before I flew to see my brother in Phoenix, I got her response:

"Holy shit go down this avenue. Let's see where it leads you. SO PROUD of you."

Hollis was decisive where I was hesitant. I realized it was because she knew how to be true to herself. The six months I spent with her taught me so much about being true to myself. Between her, Beka, and my yoga teachers, I had met so many authentic women who knew who they were and lived in alignment with their truth. They were honest and powerful.

During my marriage and after my divorce, I had become terrified of women. I hadn't taken accountability for my blunders and had blamed them all on my ex. I didn't admit that I had betrayed myself from day one with Karen and that I was equally at fault. My fear of women worsened when my best friend, Dan, went through his divorce a year after I did. In my mind, the girls Dan and I dated and married at BYU were two of the best ones, as good as any of the other girls there. If they were rotten, all women must be rotten.

Dan got divorced the same month his first baby was born, and his experience was like mine. We had done all we could in our marriages yet had failed. Viewing the world through this lens made relationships look so scary to me.

Dan held a more realistic view of relationships than I did. His attitude was if it didn't work out, it's her loss, and there are plenty more fish in the sea. We didn't talk that often about how hard our marriages had been, but sharing the common hardship of divorce brought us closer together. He hadn't been single long before he started dating again.

I was still nervous more than two years later. My sister had helped me see myself falling back into unhealthy relationship patterns after my divorce. She helped me snap out of it then. I was afraid I would go back to "that same damn place" I learned about in "The Truth about Love" seminar.

I looked back through texts Dan had sent me last summer. "Bro, you have got to start dating again," Dan had told me months earlier in the summer of 2019. "Get to it, brother!" He was an excellent cheerleader. "Love you, brother," his trademark phrase, was never far behind.

I thought back on the dates I had stumbled through two summers ago. It was time to try again. I downloaded the LDS dating app and started with the free local version. There weren't a lot of LDS girls in the South. Next thing I knew, I was swiping through girls out West. My comfort zone was still Utah and Arizona. Even after five years in Georgia, that was still *home*. There was no shortage of options in Utah! I went to Utah to see Dan and set up a date.

That first date was fun, but my feelings went haywire. I liked the girl. We went for a hike, had dinner, and each of us shared our hopes and dreams of finding a partner and getting married and having kids.

I didn't know what to do with myself after our date. I had opened the lid on a box that had been closed for years. We had planned to hang out for breakfast the next day, and then she canceled because she didn't feel well. I said I could extend my trip another day, but then I wondered if that was too much pressure.

I cried in frustration. I hadn't been on a date in two years. It was painful.

I talked to Dan.

"You need to chill out, man, she's just not into you, okay?" He brought me down to earth over our late breakfast. "I went on like ten dates last Saturday. Keep them short, just get juice, all I ever do is get a juice with them. Easy. Then if you do want to see them again, go for it. But if not, it's just juice. You're in and out in twenty minutes tops. Why be miserable and lonely if there are good girls out there waiting for you? Hotlanta, baby, there must be tons of chicks out there!"

Why had we done such a long first date? I wondered. *I set myself up for failure.*

I laughed it off after he dropped me off at the airport, still very insecure about my feelings. I had started to see how different I needed to act if I wanted to have a successful dating life. Flying across the country for a long first date was not part of the plan.

Now that I was flying West again to see my brother, I thought more about dating. I believed I was going to be moving back West, and I needed to be ready when I met my match. I needed practice. Lots and lots of practice.

I thought back over my good decisions in the past few years. I had decided to work at Imaca, even though Karen hated it. Now I made three hundred thousand a year and believed I could take this career to Phoenix. I drove a 4Runner that matched my lifestyle. I had an authentic workout routine. I had a book deal. I had a great relationship with my friends, family, and kids. I stopped throughout the day to give prayers of gratitude to God.

Good things happen when you consider *yourself* in your decisions!

Ten days after I got the book deal, I was in Phoenix with Kyle at the Cardinals vs. 49ers game. We had a blast. Phoenix felt like home. It was close to Utah, warm, full of palm trees and pretty women, close to the ocean, and large enough for me to do my job. It was the only place that made sense for me. I wanted to be there.

As soon as the trip was over, I planned another one for the tail end of Christmas Break. Kyle was doing a one-year master's degree and was nearly halfway done.

That meant I only had a few more months of a free place to stay when visiting the area. The critically acclaimed World War I movie *1917* was coming out over Christmas, and this would be a great reason to visit Kyle again. I thought, *Maybe I can fit in some dates while I am there.*

Between the trip to see Dan and the trip to see Kyle, I had done my best to heed Dan's advice. I downloaded another dating app, Hinge, and went on dozens of mini dates like Dan suggested. I was starting to feel comfortable around girls again.

I told Kyle about my idea to come back in a couple months, pitched the war movie and a hike, and he was in. I dialed in the search results to show me women in Phoenix to line up some dates for early January.

Yoga taught me that where your intention goes, your energy flows. I turned my intentions to Phoenix. I didn't know how it was possible, but I believed anyway. Like the Mother Mary card told me, I would let faith light the way.

In the first week of January, Kyle and I hiked, feasted, and footballed our way through a day-and-a-half of bro time. The evening after the war movie, I went on a fun basketball date with a girl in downtown Mesa. She was fun and athletic and pretty. We didn't talk much after, but she was the sort of girl I was looking for. I knew there would be more like her. LDS like me, athletic like me, and happy like me. Women weren't as scary anymore. I didn't see myself as the knight in shining armor anymore. I was just a guy looking for a girl I liked.

I got back to Atlanta, and my world changed quickly. I had another Reiki session with Beka, this time at her place. She told me that 2020 would be a wild year and everything would change. Some good, some bad, but everything about the world would change.

I pulled another card, from a different oracle deck, and this time it was an enchanting blonde mermaid looking off in the distance of a captivating other-worldly landscape called Mintaka. She sat on what looked like a glacier overlooking the water, her hands resting on the frozen swath of ice. Her mermaid tail swooped playfully over to the side.

"Longing for home." I read the card description as tears entered my eyes. "Belonging. The original light workers." I got chills as I read the last part.

Beka read the description from her book. "Mintakans are a soul group who originated on a planet in the constellation Orion," she read. "The Mintakan's home planet is thought to have been a water world . . . many Mintakans have an odd longing for home . . . it could mean that you are longing for a sense of belonging. Perhaps you feel this longing for home without knowing where that is . . . you are being called to create it now . . . choose where you most feel home and create it."

I had already started creating my Arizona home in my heart.

I stared at the girl on the card while Beka read. I wanted to find her. Was she somehow tied to my forgotten identity? Or was she connected to the woman I would find in Arizona? I took a picture of the card and imagined her throughout the days and weeks that followed.

"See, I said you were going to move!" Beka exclaimed after reading the card. "Any news on that yet? Or finding love?"

"Well," I replied, "you were right about finding my voice first, and now my book is getting published! I am feeling like a move will happen, but I don't know exactly how, just yet."

"Congrats on your book!" she said. "That's awesome! And on your upcoming move. You'll be home before you know it."

Home before I know it.

I liked the sound of that!

It seemed that Beka's predictions about the new year were right. 2020 came fast and hard. In late January, at the end of a running date with a girl, we noticed that everyone around us stopped and stared at their phones, almost in unison.

My heart fell to the pavement as I read that Kobe Bryant had just died in a helicopter crash. He had been my idol growing up. I learned about work ethic and mastery by watching Kobe. He was part of a game I often played. Rather than walking to trash cans, I would toss my waste at the bin, just so I could say *Kobe* if it went in. I ended the running date early. I went home and talked to friends, weeping at the hurt of feeling him go.

That afternoon I bought fifty-three copies of the first edition of his book *Mamba Mentality*. All the orders got canceled except for one. I felt so lucky to have that one copy.

My family came to town for Rex's baptism at the beginning of March. I rented a fun vehicle for us to drive around in—a new kind of throwback sports car called a Vanderhall Venice. If the Slingshot is a Batmobile, the Vanderhall is a rocket on wheels. Sleek and tubular like an old boxcar, but fast enough for the Autobahn. I drove Rex to his baptism in the convertible racecar and let him push the turbo button a few times. I wore my weightlifting gloves to grip the real walnut woodgrain steering wheel. I felt like my grandpa, who had raced boxcars in Utah.

I baptized Rex on Saturday, March 7. In many churches it's either a Pastor or a Priest who performs the baptisms. In the LDS church, any worthy Priesthood holder can do it regardless of office in the church.

Karen had sent me emails that I was not worthy to baptize him, because I was an adulterer. The bishop decided otherwise. This was the milestone event I tied to my recovery timeline in my journal three years earlier. "By Rex's baptism, I want to be married."

Where your intention goes, your energy flows.

Most of mine and Karen's immediate families came to Rex's baptism that Saturday. We were split into two sections at the church. My side was happy and loud. The Adams' side was still and silent. It was the first time we had all been in the same room since the divorce. It was the opposite of how a meeting like this would have been five years earlier. The Adams family looked sad and miserable. Nobody smiled or talked or interacted at all. They sat with blank stares. I shook everyone's hands and tried to be pleasant. Karen wanted her dad to be the one to baptize Rex. I think she legally could have made it so based on our Georgia divorce decree, since I pretty much gave her all the power. But she let it go. I was so happy to be the one to baptize my son. Rex beamed as we stood together in the waist-deep water of the baptismal font.

The boys had spent the previous two days with my family and me. After the baptism, they went with the Adams'.

I was supposed to return the Vanderhall that afternoon. It was so fun to drive that I extended my rental for another week.

My sister Kelly and I got up early on Sunday morning and went racing. Not on a racetrack, just driving fast on the highway. We cruised through Alpharetta as the brisk morning air whipped by us at speeds approaching 100 mph.

Just as the light of dawn streamed through the mammoth trees that lined the freeway, blue and red lights appeared in the rearview mirrors.

My heart sunk as I pushed in the clutch and pulled over on the wide freeway shoulder. As much as it sucked to get pulled over, it felt pretty good being in such a cool car.

"License and registration," said the officer as he approached. "Cool car, by the way. Can't say I blame you for hauling ass, but I will need to give you a ticket."

Neither of us needed him to say how fast I was going. I brushed my hand over my pockets and froze, realizing my next mistake. I didn't have my wallet. Now I was about to get two huge tickets, one for speeding and one for driving without a license. I took a deep breath and glanced at my sister as I calmed myself. *I am caught either way,* I told myself, *so I might as well enjoy it.* I was stepping into my dream life. I was in my dream car with my sister. I remembered how lucky I had gotten in New York City the year before when I refused to give my ID to the cops. I wasn't going to let this little mishap derail our morning joy ride.

I couldn't believe what I was about to say, but I leaned toward him and said it anyway.

"Officer, these are my racing clothes. I'm sorry, but I don't keep a license in my racing clothes."

I had stunned him. He was speechless. I broke the silence by assuring him that my license was valid. I told him my license number and he wrote it down.

He returned to his squad car to decide what to do with me.

"Bro, racing clothes, what the heck?" Kelly asked me, laughing. "You are a wild man. You probably should get tossed in jail for talking like that!"

"Not sure what got into me," I said, subduing my laughter while the officer was still watching us. "Really trying to find my voice these days."

In a stroke of good luck, the officer did not cite me for driving without a license. After he let us go, Kelly and I burst into laughter.

"Racing clothes!" I exclaimed. "What was I thinking? Good thing I had my license number memorized!"

I drove even faster after getting the ticket.

While I was out racing around Georgia, the world around me was shutting down. Everyone started talking about the Coronavirus. Soon it would be known as COVID-19.

I raced back South to Buckhead late in the afternoon of Monday March 9, blasting my favorite radio station as I tried to beat a rainstorm home. Between songs the hosts were talking COVID nonstop. The next day on Tuesday, March 10, emails poured in. To me, this sounded like the next Swine Flu. In the South this kind of thing happened every time there was a hurricane. Every fall. Everyone would rush to get food, gas, and bottled water. Panic would sink in. Inevitably the storm would pass and everything would return to normal.

Later that day, Imaca HR sent an email confirming the baseless havoc. "While there is still more to learn about Coronavirus, normal sick policies are in effect." To me, that meant *It's going to blow over soon, keep on working and don't worry about it.*

Imaca was in the middle of upgrading their headquarters and moving into one of the largest office buildings in Utah County. It was business as usual.

That Friday, I held a call with our Head of Legal and an international businessman. He used words and phrases like "quarantine" and "COVID test" and "essential business" and "airport masks." I realized this was *not* another Swine Flu. It was global. America was in the beginning stages of what other countries had dealt with for months. This pandemic would change things for everyone.

I had no idea. The emails kept pouring in over the weekend. No international travel. Video calling became the new way to have meetings. "Work from home" became the most popular subject line in my inbox.

The Monday after Rex's baptism, March 16, Atlanta Public Schools announced that schools would close for the rest of the semester. I saw the opening I had been waiting for. This sounded like my opportunity to get to Arizona and find my dream life.

The next morning, I got word from Imaca. I could now work from home at my discretion. I would still travel some, but not every week like before. It was up to me. *Up to me.* I could work from Timbuktu or Kathmandu if I wanted to. Everything was flexible. My work could now be done virtually. From anywhere. Mother Mary's miracle was gaining momentum quickly!

Deep feelings bubbled to the surface. My three-year divorce timeline was waning. That magical manifestation I promised myself two years and eleven months ago was only one month away. Preschool was over, alimony was almost over, Karen was almost done with her PhD, Rex had turned eight and was baptized. Even though we were still stuck in Atlanta and Karen was getting married in a few months, the possibility of possibilities grew stronger. I was ready for a new life. I was ready to find love. It was time to go.

Tuesday night, March 17, I couldn't sleep. I wrote in my memoir and thought about moving to Arizona. Palm trees, warm weather, and the woman on the other side of the Mother Mary card. The mystery woman I had seen again on the Mintaka card.

At five a.m., I went to the closet and pulled out the pair of Brooks Ghost running shoes I bought on eBay after reading *Can't Hurt Me.* If David Goggins could do ten thousand pull ups, I could move to Arizona. I was nervous about instigating this huge change. I needed to put all my nerves to good use. I decided to run a route I had been considering. It amounted to just over twenty-one miles, with no water, and no breaks.

Later I would learn that on the other side of the country someone else had also been up most of the night. We had not yet met, but when we did, learning how our timelines wove together would become a meaningful part of our love story.

The very day I decided to move to Arizona to find my family was the day of her birthday. Little did I know her birthday wish was to have a family again. Like me, she woke up early on March 18 and imagined life with a real and honest partner. Like me, she took a long break from dating and socializing, going inward to find out what hurt the most and find healing, without looking around for someone to fix her.

We had not met, and would not meet for six more months, but that morning, our souls united. We did not know it yet, but that day began our journey into each other's arms.

As I ran that morning, I ran for the courage to travel west. I ran for the power of love. I began to trust that I was worthy of love and happiness. I started to believe that I could have what I wanted. I ran that morning to break free of my past limits and lies, and to prove to myself that anything was possible.

I had never seen Atlanta's morning rats before. They were everywhere. I ran past the lions in front of the JW Marriott and knocked on the metal light post outside the Greyhound station by the old Braves stadium. Time to turn around. As I ran back up Peachtree, a thick fog appeared with the rising light of dawn. My legs were on wings as I cruised to my Northern marker and then back to my condo. The magic of the runner's high had set in. I felt like I could Forrest Gump it all the way to Arizona. I felt like I could do anything.

But I was nervous. Making big decisions was not my strong suit. I picked an incompatible spouse and stayed miserable in our relationship for seven years. I chose a college degree with little practical application to my life. Every time I tried a relationship, I ruined it. My fears mounted. How could I trust myself? What if this whole thing backfired? What if Karen got upset and retaliated? What if Imaca changed us to full travel again, didn't approve my proposed transfer, and I got fired? What if I couldn't sell my condo?

I took a deep cleansing breath and my fears dissolved. My joy was worth the risk. I called Karen and asked if I could take the boys to my parents' house in Utah for quarantine.

She said yes without hesitation.

She told me the boys were in Chattanooga at Ron's parents' house for the week. I was so happy she said yes, I didn't argue with her for sending the boys out-of-state to stay with people I had never met, without my consent. We agreed that on Friday I would pick them up and we would be off to Utah.

That night I wanted to scream and dance with excitement. But part of me was still afraid. Afraid that even after all the miracles of the past months, it wouldn't work. My victory would be short-lived. I would end up back in Georgia. I caught myself worrying and decided to celebrate enough to at least have my favorite meal. I walked down Pharr Road and picked up Thai coconut chicken soup with spring rolls and extra peanut sauce.

I brought it back to my condo and gazed out over the flickering city lights while I ate. A meal I had eaten dozens of times in this condo, now for the last time. I calmed myself and dreamt of eating with my Mintakan mermaid. I would find her. I would make it to her in Arizona.

The next day, what I hoped was my last day as an Atlanta resident, I hopped on some local online marketplaces and picked up essentials for our trip: Nerf guns, frisbees, balls, and boomerangs. I packed our essentials and picked up the boys in Chattanooga on Friday.

We arrived at my parents' house in Kanab on Sunday night.

I did it! The boys were with me, back west, with no plans to return to Georgia.

I hoped the boys wouldn't end up having to go back to Atlanta. Karen's PhD course work would be over in a few months. I had no idea what she planned to do for work, but she had all sorts of stories she told me. She was selling something to Google, doing something with Uber, working on something for Target. I had been married to her long enough to know these tall tales were likely nothing more than fantasies. For most of 2019, she had tried to convince me she was going to work for the FBI and that I would need to take care of the boys while she trained at Quantico. Nothing ever came of it. I did not trust her stories. They reminded me of the stories she told others while we were married, how she was often getting certified, something I had never heard of. I smiled and nodded. These were her stories.

There was still her engagement to Ron. That I knew was real. How would that play into everything? It was already March, and the announcement she sent me was for an August wedding. I stopped worrying and tried to stay curious. Somehow it would work out.

Before I went to bed that Sunday, I read the same line of scripture that had comforted me when I was broke with a huge tax bill and a broken car in 2017: "With God all things are possible." At five a.m. on Monday morning after we arrived, I kept up my routine and went running. In January I had decided to run a fifty-miler for my birthday that year. I was training like crazy to be ready.

After my run I approached the freezing cold front screen door at my parents' house. I hesitated to grab it and push the top thumb button down because I knew how cold it would be. As I reached out and I pressed it, I heard a voice, as if I had pressed a button on an intercom. The voice said: "You are home now, and here you will stay."

I remembered the previous night, "With God all things are possible."

I believed the voice. I knew it was true. Somehow, the boys and I were Arizona-bound. This was my Mintaka. My home. The full picture wasn't yet clear, but I had faith, allowing myself to believe I'd made it. Waiting anxiously for the details to work out.

I hadn't spoken to Karen since we arrived in Kanab. I had the boys call her with updates, but I kept myself out of it. When she called me for the first time the morning of April 1, my stomach tightened. As her name flashed on the home screen of the phone buzzing next to me, I wondered why she was calling. I believed my path to Arizona would soon appear. Our joint custody meant that meant she would need to be a part of it.

"Hello," I answered quickly.

"Hey Matt!" she responded. "From what the boys have told me you have been pretty busy out there!"

"Yeah, we made it out here, safe and sound, the boys are back doing online school and lots of outdoors adventures," I said.

"They are growing up so fast. Quarantine in Kanab! Who would have thought? Thanks again for supporting me in this. The boys are loving it."

"You bet," she replied. "Yes, quarantine is totally crazy."

I wasted no time.

"Hey, I know you and Ron are settling down out there, but driving back here in a time of emergency helped me realize how much I miss the west," I said. "It sure would be nice to make it back out here someday. Do you think that could ever be part of the plan?"

"Actually, yes!" she exclaimed, catching me off guard with her enthusiasm. "Things aren't working out with me and Ron anymore. I met a guy from Phoenix last fall, well, I met him before that, but we started dating last fall. He offered me a job, and we're planning to get engaged this summer. Do you think Phoenix could work?"

What? How could she steal my thunder like that? I had known Arizona would happen, but this was too fast even for me. She was trading in her fiancé of two years for a different one across the country as if it were an Amazon return.

I tried to say something. Nothing was there. I was speechless.

"Does Ron know?" was all I could come up with.

"No, not yet."

This made sense, considering she had just used Ron's parents in Chattanooga as free babysitters at the onset of COVID.

We reversed roles from what I had anticipated on this whole moving thing. Suddenly, *she* was the one trying to convince *me* to move. And, exactly where I wanted to move. This was unbelievable. I felt conflicted.

On the one hand, I heard the sad tale of one guy about to have his heart broken by his fiancée, with my little boys caught in the middle. On the other hand, Mother Mary was granting my wish and using this tragedy to help me pull off a miracle move across the country in the middle of a global pandemic. As much as I believed Karen's plan would soon fall apart, I knew this was what I had been praying for.

Her news brought up my unresolved feelings of guilt from our divorce. Now seeing this terrible choice she was making, becoming engaged to someone new without even telling her fiancé, and brushing it off as if it were nothing. I caught a glimpse of the sort of chaos I had saved myself from. I felt less guilty about divorcing her.

But I felt bad for Ron, who I'd been exchanging kids with for an entire year. Karen had been busy *working.* Apparently, she had been on personal business in Phoenix. With her new fiancé. The guy who my boys called "Ron Dad," was out. This new guy was in.

Had I caused this? Did asking for a miracle mean someone else had to suffer?

And then I realized . . . if this was how she treated Ron, he didn't deserve this either. My miracle could save both of us. And why was I so worried about him anyway? Falling back into old patterns. Always trying to make others happy. Afraid to ask for what I wanted, and fight for it, for fear of disturbing someone else.

No. That stopped now. Karen wanted Phoenix, and that was a miracle. Because I wanted Phoenix too.

I stopped trying to understand her side of it and stepped back into my side of the story.

"So, Phoenix?" I uttered encouragingly. Even though her plan was fraught with issues and drama, and even though I knew she may change her mind later, I went for it. I needed to act fast before her plans blew up.

"I think I need until fall to get out there, but let's plan on the boys starting school in Phoenix this fall," Karen continued.

She had already planned it out. Phoenix was materializing right before my eyes, and I didn't even have to fight for it. As she told me more about her plans, I wondered how this had happened.

Karen told me exactly what I wanted to hear without me saying a word. I was ecstatic and awestruck. She would have doubts. She would change her mind. Her relationship with this new fiancé would probably end, and then she would want to move back to Atlanta. That was what I heard in the middle of all her, "He said he will buy me a house," and "He's offering to make me a partner in his business," and "He has three kids, and we are taking all the kids to Disney in July."

"Sounds good," I said, keeping it short. "I'll sell my place and find one down there, and we'll be settled by August. Can you send me some of the ideas you guys have for school options, where I should look for a house, et cetera?"

"Oh sure," she said. "Joe is well connected. His kids go to a school that is by invitation only, and he can put in a word for the boys. He's in Queen Creek, but it's right next to Gilbert, Mesa, and Chandler, lots of options."

I made sure to confirm these items with her via text and save the screenshots.

Just like that, it was settled. We were moving to Arizona. One big happy divorced family wanting the same move.

The boys and I stepped fully into the best summer of our lives in Kanab while transitioning down the highway to Arizona.

The last piece of the puzzle was my job. I had purposely put this off. There was one obvious choice, which was VP of the West Coast, as I had been VP of the Southeast. That position had been held by my boss and friend Matt Kennedy for years. He had wanted to give it up and had asked for my help to vet candidates several times. Finally, as part of the COVID announcements, our CEO announced he was moving out of field work and into a consulting role. It was another pinch-me moment. Timing seemed to work out beautifully in my favor. But still, I was nervous.

How could I be nervous? Mother Mary had carried me across the country. She had canceled an ex-wife's engagement for me and arranged a new one in the exact metropolis where I wanted to move. How could I doubt?

I spent the week after Karen called mustering the courage to call my CEO.

"Hey Arron," I choked out through the flutter of butterflies in my stomach. "COVID finally opened things up for me to move back West, with Kennedy moving on can I have his spot? I'm out here now but can keep working the Region for now to smooth out the transition and find a replacement."

"September would work better for us. Does September work for you?" he asked.

"Yes," I replied. "September is perfect!"

"Sounds good, thanks! Bye, Matt."

It was done. Everyone had told me what I wanted to hear. As I thought of Mother Mary and Mintaka, I smiled from pinky finger to pinky finger.

This was the pattern COVID-19 set for me: "I will shut down the world for you and cancel the little plans you've distracted yourself with so you can accomplish your dreams."

I opened my journal and looked at my next few months' calendar. We had the Bahamas booked for my birthday: canceled. Mexico booked for mid-May: canceled. Graduations to attend in Arizona and Washington: canceled. Rim-to-rim run the Grand Canyon: also canceled. I couldn't believe how much time and energy I had planned to spend on things that didn't help me accomplish my goals. It was time for a reset.

I traded in "trip to Bahamas" for "sell condo in Atlanta."

I traded in "trip to Mexico" for "find home in Arizona."

I traded in "train for Grand Canyon run" for "start finding girls to date in Arizona."

I held the bright image of the Mintakan mermaid high in my mind. She was so close now I could feel it. Had I already crossed her path? If not, I soon would.

I flipped back to the beginning of my journal where I wrote my one-page, three-year divorce recovery plan in the Spring of 2017. I had finally made it to the end. Three years earlier, my days felt slow and gray, like an old newspaper. Over the past year, I started to see my life through new and eager eyes. My life became as fast and flexible as online ordering.

The pandemic-frozen world stood still while I leapt fearlessly into the future. A future I had long awaited, where my dreams were finally about to come true.

About the Author

MATT OMEGA GREW UP IN THE RED ROCK SANCtuary of Kanab, Utah, the oldest of five kids, playing football and writing news stories. He served an LDS mission in 2007–2009 and met his first wife shortly after while attending BYU. After six years of marriage and with two young sons, Matt made the difficult decision to divorce. The three transformative years that followed became the heart of this book.

In 2020, Matt found love again and, in May 2021, married his twin soul, Alissa Omega, beneath a lunar eclipse at the base of Mauna Kea in Kona, Hawaii. Together, they chose the last name "Omega," drawn not from bloodlines, but from belonging. A name that symbolizes unity in their own blended family, and their belief that all humankind is one big family longing to come home to that same kind of oneness.

Matt and Alissa share five boys and one daughter together and live in Mesa, Arizona. They host a live show on YouTube most Tuesday evenings called Alpha to Omega: Conversations for a New Earth.

Matt enjoys writing, the outdoors, and meaningful conversation. He's currently working in fintech while supporting Alissa in building her home-based quantum healing practice, Omega Heart Healing. He's currently finishing his third memoir and writing his first children's book.

www.ingramcontent.com/pod-product-compliance
Lightning Source LLC
Chambersburg PA
CBHW062212080426
42734CB00010B/1865